SKETCHES OF CEYLON HISTORY

SKETCHES
OF
CEYLON HISTORY

P. ARUNACHALAM

SECOND EDITION

REVISED WITH MAPS AND ILLUSTRATIONS

GYAN

Published by

Gyan Publishing House
5, Ansari Road
Daryaganj, New Delhi-110002
Phone: 011-47034999, 9811692060
E-mail: books@gyanbooks.com

Distribution Network
gyanbooks.com
India, USA, Canada, UK, Australia, France

ISBN : 9788121240291 (PB)
First Published, Colombo, 1906

2nd Impression 2020

Printed at: Gyan Press, Delhi.

Sketches of Ceylon History
Author: P. Arunachalam

SKETCHES
OF
CEYLON HISTORY

BY

P. ARUNACHALAM, M.A. Cantab.

Barrister-at-law, Lincoln's Inn; Ceylon Civil Service;

Member of the Ceylon Legislative Council.

2ND EDITION,

REVISED, WITH MAPS AND ILLUSTRATIONS.

Colombo:

PRINTED BY THE COLOMBO APOTHECARIES CO., LTD.,

1906.

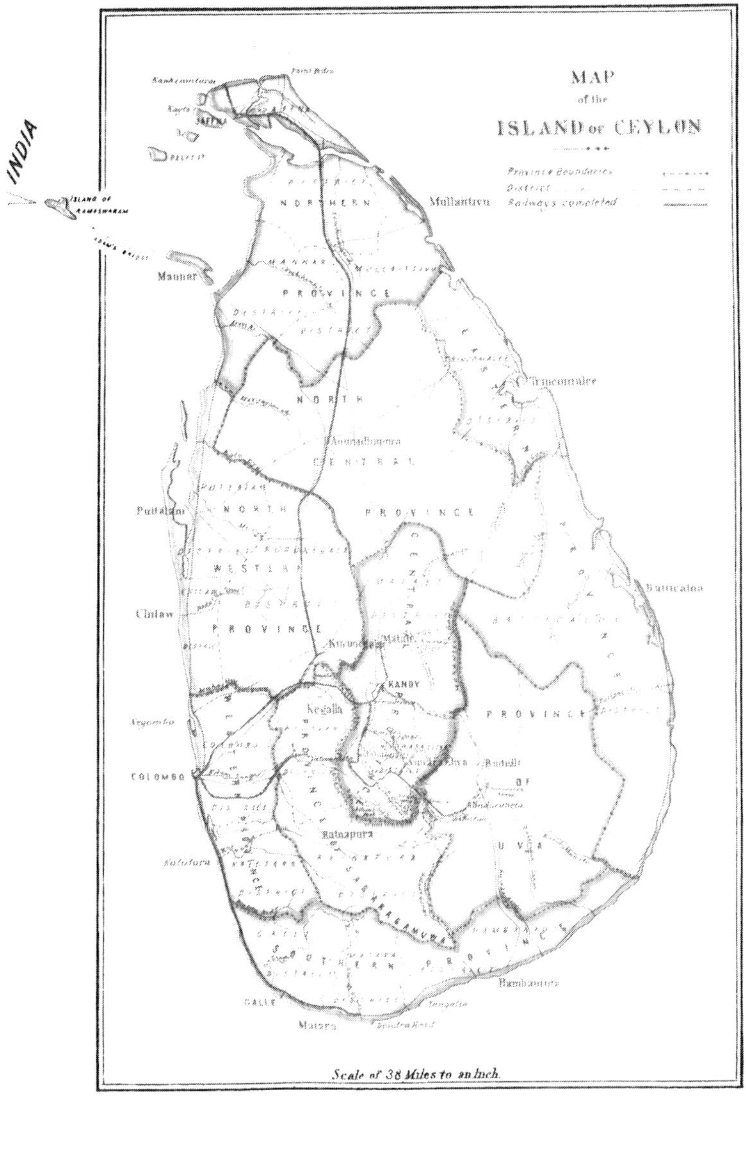
MAP
of the
ISLAND of CEYLON
Province Boundaries
District
Railways completed
INDIA
ISLAND OF RAMESWARAM
JAFFNA
Manaar
NORTHERN PROVINCE
NORTH CENTRAL PROVINCE
NORTH WESTERN PROVINCE
CENTRAL
PROVINCE OF UVA
SOUTHERN PROVINCE
Puttalam
Chilaw
Negombo
COLOMBO
Kalutara
GALLE
Matara
Kegalla
KANDY
Ratnapura
Badulla
Batticaloa
Hambantota
Trincomalee
Scale of 38 Miles to an Inch.

PREFACE.

The substance of these Sketches was delivered, on the 30th January last, as a lecture, at which His Excellency the Governor was pleased to preside. It was published in the *Ceylon National Review* at the time, and also as a separate edition. The edition was soon exhausted and a second edition called for. I have taken the opportunity to revise and enlarge it and add maps, illustrations and an index.

The growing interest in the history of our country is a sign of the times. It is a satisfaction to know that His Excellency does not approve of the exclusion of Ceylon History from the curriculum of our English schools, and that the defect will shortly be remedied.

P. ARUNACHALAM.

August 15, 1906,
Colombo.

Maps.

Illustrations.

Lists of Kings.

Index.

SKETCHES OF CEYLON HISTORY.

I.

THE history of Ceylon is a subject about which many of us can hardly be said to be burdened with much knowledge. We know a great deal about the history of England and of ancient Rome. Our children can tell us all about the Norman Conquest, the Peloponnesian War, the capitals of English and Scotch counties, the capes and rivers of South America, the manufactories of Chicago. But of the elements of Ceylon geography and history they are in blissful ignorance. Many even of our educated men have but a dim idea of who Sanghamitta was or Mahinda, Dutugemunu or Elala, what associations cluster round Mahiyangana or Munissaram, Aluvihara or Kataragama, what was the origin and history of cloth manufacture in the Island or of the coco-palm. Kotte and Sitawaka, in comparatively recent times, witnessed the heroic resistance of our people and kings to foreign invaders from generation to generation. The names of these places waken no emotion in our hearts. We think of Kotte mainly as the suburb which supplies the children of Colombo with nurses. Sitawaka, rich not only in the memories of this struggle but in the romance of Queen Sita's captivity and rescue in a bygone millennium, is lost in the unromantic tea-district of Avissawella. Robert Knox, a little over two centuries ago, spent many years of captivity in Ceylon, little dreaming of the destiny that awaited his countrymen here, and has recorded his experiences in one of the most interesting works in English literature. Few read the book, fewer still know the spot where he lived in captivity and buried his father.

It is scarcely creditable to us to remain in such profound ignorance of the history of our Mother-land

and to be so indifferent to our past and surroundings. It is a great loss, for not only is the history of Ceylon among the oldest, most interesting and fascinating in the world, going back twenty-four centuries, but no people can break with its past as we are trying to do. It has been truly said: 'A people without a past is as a ship without ballast.' How dreary, too, is the life of many of our educated men and women, with eyes fixed and ideals formed on Bayswater and Clapham, and their intellectual food trashy novels and magazines! No wonder that visitors to this beautiful Island are struck with the absence of originality, of organic life, in our people.

There are signs, however, that the dark fog in which we are content to remain will lift ere long. It is refreshing to read a Royal College boy protesting in the College Magazine against the exclusion of Ceylon history and geography from the curriculum of our leading schools. Some time ago the officers of a public department in Colombo formed themselves into a society for the promotion of historic study and research. They used to read together and discuss the *Mahâwansa*, the ancient chronicles of Ceylon, a veritable storehouse of valuable information, of which there is an excellent translation by Turnour and Wijesinha. Each member was also expected to acquaint himself with all matters of antiquarian or scientific interest in his native village or town and to communicate and discuss them at meetings of the Society. The plan is one which might with benefit be generally adopted.

Rich treasures of history, ethnology, folklore, botany, geology, zoology await the explorer in every part of the Island. Our educated men and women can hardly do better than devote some of their leisure to this exploration, working in co-operation at various centres, discussing the results at local meetings and in journals such as that of the Royal Asiatic Society. It is work that any intelligent person, however limited his sphere and opportunities, can take part in. It would give a new zest to our life and surroundings, would furnish abundant material to the *R. A. S. Journal*, now almost dying of starvation, and would lay the foundation for a much-needed comprehensive and up-to-date account of Ceylon—physical, historical and topographical.

It would help also to recall to us and fix in our minds the great things done by our ancestors. Thus we may in time recover some of our lost originality and acquire that self-confidence which is indispensable to national progress and national success. It is our good fortune to live under a Government which will foster every attempt in this direction. In a speech recently delivered by the Lord-Lieutenant of Ireland he happily expressed the imperial policy of Britain.

"There are some people," he said, "who seem to believe that the only way in which a great Empire can be successfully maintained is by suppressing the various distinct elements of its component parts, in fact by running it as a huge regiment in which each nation is to lose its individuality and to be brought under a common system of discipline and drill. In my opinion, we are much more likely to break up an Empire than to maintain it by any such attempt. Lasting strength and loyalty are not to be secured by any attempt to force into one system or to remould into one type those special characteristics which are the outcome of a nation's history and of her religious and social conditions, but rather by a full recognition of the fact that these very characteristics form an essential part of a nation's life and that under wise guidance and under sympathetic treatment they will enable her to provide her own contribution and to play her special part in the life of the Empire to which she belongs."

II.

The primitive history of Ceylon is enveloped in fable, yet there is perhaps no country in the world that has such a long continuous history and civilization. At a time when the now great nations of the West were sunk in barbarism, or had not yet come into existence, Ceylon was the seat of an ancient kingdom and religion, the nursery of art, and the centre of Eastern commerce. Her stupendous religious edifices more than 2,000 years old and, in extent and architectural interest, second only to the structures of Egypt, and her vast irrigation works, attest the greatness and antiquity of her civilization. Her rich products of nature and art, the beauty of her scenery, her fame as the home of a pure Buddhism, have made her from remote times the object of interest and admiration to contemporary nations. Merchants, sailors, and pilgrims have in diverse tongues left records of their visits, which confirm in a striking manner the ancient native chronicles which Ceylon is almost singular among Asiatic lands in possessing.

Ceylon, it is believed, was part of the region of Ophir and Tarshish of the Hebrews, from which king Solomon's navy supplied him with "gold and silver, ivory, and apes and peacocks." * To the ancient Greeks and Romans the Island was known by the name of Taprobane, by which name it is described by Onesicritus, Diodorus Siculus, Ovid, Strabo, Pliny, Ptolemy and others—a name, too, familiar to English readers through Milton :

> "Embassies from regions far remote,
> From India and the golden Chersonese,
> And utmost Indian isle, Taprobane."

* 1 *Kings*, *X.*, *22.*—The Hebrew word used for peacock (*tuki*) is unmistakably the Tamil word *tokei*, while the word for apes (*kapi*) is the Sanskrit and Tamil *kapi* and the word for ivory (*shen habbim* the tooth of the *habb*) is the Sanskrit *ibham* and Tamil *ibam*.

The name is another form of "Tamba-panni," one of the names given to Ceylon in the Sinhalese chronicles. It is explained in the *Mahawansa* * (I., p. 33) as derived from *tamba-pánayó* (copper-palmed), having been given to the Island by Wijaya and his followers, who, "exhausted by sea-sickness and faint from weakness, had landed out of the vessel supporting themselves on the palms of their hands pressed on the ground........hence their palms became copper-coloured" *(tambapánayó).* A fanciful explanation. On the opposite coast of India there is a river still called Támraparni, and the name may have been brought to Ceylon by the early Tamil settlers, a common practice among colonists in ancient and modern times. Vergil in his *Æneid* makes Æneas, on landing in Italy, express surprise at seeing a little Troy, another Pergamus and another river Xanthus.

> "Parvam Trojam simulataque magnis
> Pergama et arentem Xanthi cognomine rivum
> Adgnosco."†

How many English and Scotch names of places have been introduced into Ceylon by British colonists!

The Arabs called Ceylon "Serendib" and the Portuguese "Ceilao." The names are probably derived from *Sinhala* or *Sihalam* (changed to *Selan* and *Seren*) and *Dwipa* (an Island) changed to *dib*. To the inhabitants of the neighbouring continent of India it was known centuries before the Christian era by the name of *Lanka* (the resplendent), the name it still bears among the native inhabitants, both Sinhalese and Tamil. The Siamese have added the honorific Tewa, calling the Island *Tewa Lanka*, "divine Lanka." To the Chinese Ceylon was "the Island of jewels," to

* Translation of Turnour and Wijesingha, published by the Government Printer, Ceylon, 1889.

† *Verg. Æneid*, III., 349.

the Greeks "the land of the hyacinth and the ruby," to the Indian Buddhist "the pearl upon the brow of India."

The traditions respecting the Island are many and curious. The orthodox Buddhist believes that every one of the four Buddhas of the present cycle, from Kakusanda to Gautama, visited Ceylon and instructed its inhabitants, and that Gautama Buddha left on Adam's Peak his footprint as an undying memorial of his third and last visit. The Hindus claim the footprint as that of Siva, whose shrine was probably established there or revived by Samana or Lakshmana, one of the heroes of the Ramayana and the reputed guardian of the peak. From him it was called Sumana-kuta even prior to the visit of the second Buddha,* and is still called Samanala by the Sinhalese. The Mohammedans, continuing a tradition inherited from some of the early Christians, are equally positive that the footprint is that of Adam, and that Ceylon was the cradle of the human race, the Elysium provided for Adam and Eve to console them for the loss of Eden,—a tradition which somewhat softened the bitterness of the exile of Arabi Pasha and his fellow Egyptians during their internment in the Island from 1883 to 1901.

The earliest Indian tradition about Ceylon is recorded in the *Skanda Purána*, the story of the rise and fall of a mighty and wicked Titan, for whose overthrow Skanda or Kartikeya, the god of war and wisdom, was incarnated. The echoes of that contest live in a remote forest-shrine in the south-eastern corner of the Island, called after him Kartikeya Gráma or Kataragama, where after his victory he wooed and won a chieftain's daughter, who shares with him the worship of millions from Cashmere to Ceylon, and with whom the Sinhalese priests (*kapurálas*) of the

* *Maháwansa*, I., p. 58.

ADAM'S PEAK FROM MASKELIYA.

shrine proudly claim kinship. The southern bank of the Kalutara river near its mouth (Kalutara South railway station) is still locally called *Vélápura*, "the city of the lance-god," (the lance, *vel*, being his favourite weapon), and marks the limit of his territory, while the opposite bank of the river is assigned to his enemies, and is called *Désestara*, a corruption of Dévasatru (the enemies of the gods).

The next Indian tradition, later by many centuries, is that of the *Rámáyana*, the celebrated epic of Valmiki, which relates the abduction of Sita, a North Indian queen, by Rávana, King of Ceylon, the invasion of Ceylon by her husband Rama, and her recovery after a sanguinary war and the slaughter of Rávana. The bridge said to have been constructed for the passage of Rama's army to Ceylon is the Adam's Bridge of English maps. It touches the Island of Rameswaram, where, on his return from Ceylon, Rama established a shrine to Siva,—perhaps the most frequented of all the sacred spots in India,—and over which and Adam's Bridge a railway will at no distant date run, linking India and Ceylon in closer bonds. At Munissaram, in the Chilaw District, already an ancient (*mun*) shrine of Siva (*Isvara*), as its name implies, Rama is said to have worshipped on his way to battle with Rávana. The purity of Sita's character and her devotion to her husband have made her the national heroine, as he is the national hero, of India. Thousands still pass in reverent pilgrimage over their route to Ceylon. Sita's name lives in Ceylon in Sita-talawa (Sita's plain), Sita-ela (Sita's stream) and Sita-kunt (Sita's pond) between Nuwara Eliya and Hakgala, where she is said to have been confined by Rávana, and in Sitawaka (Avissawella).

Both the *Skanda Purána* and the *Rámáyana* represent Ceylon as a huge continent, a tradition not unsupported by science. The geology and fauna of the Island point to a time when Ceylon was part of an

Oriental Continent, which stretched in unbroken land from Madagascar to the Malay Archipelago and northwards to the present valley of the Ganges. The valley was then occupied by a sea spreading westward across Persia, Arabia, and the Sahara Desert, and forming the southern limit of the Palæ-arctic Continent, which embraced Europe, North Africa and North Asia. In the course of ages the greater part of the Oriental Continent was submerged in the sea, leaving Ceylon as a fragment in the centre, with, on one side, the Maldives, Laccadives, Seychelles, Mauritius, and Madagascar, themselves separated from one another by hundreds of miles of sea, and, on the other, the Malay Islands; while the Ganges valley was upheaved, making North and South India one land and, later, Ceylon itself was separated from South India by a narrow sea.

The greater part of Ceylon is said in the *Rámáyana* to have been submerged in the sea in punishment of Ravana's misdeeds, and the Great Basses Light-house, which stands out on a solitary rock in the south-east sea of Ceylon, is still called Ravana's fort. The meridian of Lanka of the Indian astronomers, which was reputed to pass through Ravana's capital, passes through the Maldive Islands at 75° 53′ 15″ East Greenwich, quite four hundred miles from the present western limit of Ceylon. On this coast the Sinhalese chronicles record extensive submersion by the sea in the reigns of Panduwasa (*circa* 500 B.C.) and Kelani Tissa (200 B.C.) At this latter period Kelani is said to have been at a distance of "seven *gaus*" (28 miles) from the sea. "The guardian deities of Lanka having become indignant," (says the *Rájávaliya*) "with Tissa, King of Kelaniya, (for the unjust execution of a Buddhist Elder), the sea began to encroach. 100,000*

* The chronicler's exaggeration, no doubt. The *Rájávaliya* is much inferior in value to the *Maháwansa*, regarding which see *infra* p. 29.

trading villages (*Patunugam*), 970 fishers' villages, and 470 villages of pearl fishers, making altogether eleven-twelfths of Lanka, were submerged by the great sea. Mannar escaped destruction: of sea-port towns Katupiti Madampe."

III.

The first historical event recorded in the chronicles is the landing of Wijaya, the discarded scion of a royal race in Northern India and the founder of the first known dynasty in Ceylon. This event is assigned to the year 544 B.C.,* about the time that Cyrus, the founder of the Persian Empire, permitted the captive Jews to return from Babylonia to Jerusalem. Over the period that intervened between the invasion of Rama and the arrival of Wijaya and which according to the Sinhalese traditions covered about 1,844 years, an impenetrable darkness hangs.

It has been usual to regard Wijaya and his followers as arriving in Ceylon from Bengal. There is hardly any warrant for this belief beyond the fact that his grandmother was a princess of Wanga (Bengal). The traditions reported in the ancient chronicles of the *Dipawansa* and *Maháwansa* point rather to Guzerat in the Bombay Presidency as his country of origin and departure. The Princess of Bengal is reputed to have run away from home and joined a caravan, and while travelling in a wilderness in the "Lala-rata," (the old name of Guzerat) was carried off by "a lion," probably a bandit of the woods, with whom she lived in a cave, bearing him a son and a daughter. When they grew up, they ran away with their mother. The lion roamed the villages, to the terror of the inhabitants, in search of his offspring and was finally slain by the son himself,

* The date of Wijaya's arrival is said by the Buddhist chroniclers to have occurred on the day of Gautama Buddha's death, which event tradition fixes at 544 B.C., but which more probably occurred about 478 B.C. For reasons see *Cunningham's Inscriptions of Asoka.*

a feat which is said to have earned for him and his descendants their name of Sinhala, the lion-slayer.* He then established himself as king of "Lala-rata," and Wijaya was his eldest son. He "became a lawless character" and had to be expelled by the king with 700 of his comrades and their wives and children. The ships containing the women and children drifted to "Nagadipa" and "Mahilarata," probably the modern Laccadive and Maldive Islands. The men landed at "Barukachcha," the modern Broach in the Bombay Presidency, and at "Suppáraka," the modern Surat, and at both ports so misbehaved that they had to be expelled by the inhabitants. They took ship again and landed at last at "Tambapanni" in Ceylon. This port is located by some on the north-western coast near Puttalam, and by others on the south-eastern coast, at the mouth of the Kirinde-Oya. The Dutch historian Valentyn placed it in Tamblegam (of Trincomalie district,) the seaport of Tamankaduwa and in old times called Tamanatota.

At the time that Wijaya arrived in Ceylon, it was inhabited by one or more races called Yakkhas and Nágas, of whom very little is known. They were a branch of a prehistoric, probably Dravidian, race which colonized South India and Ceylon. The term Yaksha, which is the Sanskrit original of "Yakkha," is in the *Rámáyana* and other Indian traditions applied to a race of spirits whose chief was Kuvera, king of Lanka, who was dispossessed by his half-brother, the famous Rávana, and is now regarded as the regent of the Northern quarter of the world and as the god of wealth. The Yakshas were akin to, if not identical with, the Nágas, the Dragon race. They appear to have attained a high state of civilization, and the names of Nagapatam in the Madras Presidency, of Nagpore in the

* The Sinhalese thus trace their origin to a lion, as the Romans of old traced theirs to twins nurtured by a wolf.

Central Provinces of India and of the Nága hills, the north-easterly offshoot of the Himàlayas, attest the wide extent of the ancient Nága dominion. Long before the Wijayan invasion Mahiyangana (now called Alutnuwara) in the Bintenna division of Uva had been one of their chief cities, and Gautama Buddha on his first visit to Ceylon is said to have descended on "the agreeable Mahanaga garden, in the assembling place of the Yakkhas,"—a site marked by the ruins of a great dagoba built about 300 B.C., and still a great place of Buddhist pilgrimage. It was the *Maagrammum* of Ptolemy, who describes it as "the metropolis of Taprobane beside the great river" (Mahaweliganga). The modern representatives of this ancient race are the fast dwindling Veddas or wild men of Ceylon and the Bhils, Santals and other wild tribes of India.

Wijaya on his arrival married (under circumstances† which recall the meeting of Ulysses and Circe in the *Odyssey*) Kuveni, a Yakkha princess of great beauty and much influence among her countrymen. With her aid he suppressed the Yakkhas and established his power, fixing his capital at Tambapanni, also called Tammana nuwara. He then basely discarded her for a Tamil princess of South India. Kuveni, seeking refuge among her own people whom she had betrayed, was killed by them. Another tradition says that the deserted queen flung herself, with curses on her husband, from a rock called after her Yakdessa gala ("the rock of the Yakkha's curse"), and which is one of the hills that give picturesqueness to the town of Kurunegala. Tonigala, "the rock of lamentations," and Vilakatupota, "the vale of tears," both in the Kurunegala District, are also associated with her sorrows.

Kuveni Asna, which relates the story of her love and sorrows, says that in agonizing shrieks she wailed:

† *Mahâwansa*, I., pp. 32, 33; and *Odyssey*, X, 274 *et seq.*

"When shipwrecked and forlorn, I found thee and thy men food and home. I helped thee to rout the Yakkhas and raised thee to be king. Pledging me thy troth, thou madest me thy spouse. Didst not thou know then, that I was of the Yakkha race? Loving thee with unquenchable love and living in such love, I bore thee children. How canst thou leave me and love another? The gentle rays of the rising full moon are now to me the blaze of a red-hot ball of iron; the cool spicy breezes of the sandal groves are hot and unwelcome; the cuckoo's sweet song pierces my ears as with a spear. Alas, how shall I soothe my bleeding heart!"

IV.

Wijaya's successors, like him, were adherents of the Brahminical faith, and took their consorts from the ancient and powerful Pandyan dynasty of South India, whose sovereigns, from their enlightened encouragement of literature, have been called the Ptolemies of India. The alliance was indispensable for the development of Ceylon, and was probably the justification of Wijaya's ingratitude to the Yakkha queen.

The cultivation of rice was among the first cares of king Wijaya. The grain was then not grown in Ceylon. When first entertained by the ill-fated queen Kuveni, he is said in the chronicles* to have been served with rice gathered from the wrecks of ships. Even 250 years later the production of rice was so limited that king Dewanampiyatissa is said to have received from the Emperor Asoka of Northern India 160 loads of hill paddy.† The Tamils, however, on the main-land had made great advance in rice cultivation. A branch of the Vellalas, the old ruling caste of Tamil-land, claims to have received the grain and instruction in its cultivation from the goddess Parvati,§ and still

* *Mahâwansa*, I., p. 33.

† *Mahâwansa*, I., p. 46.

§ Consort of Siva and also called Uma.

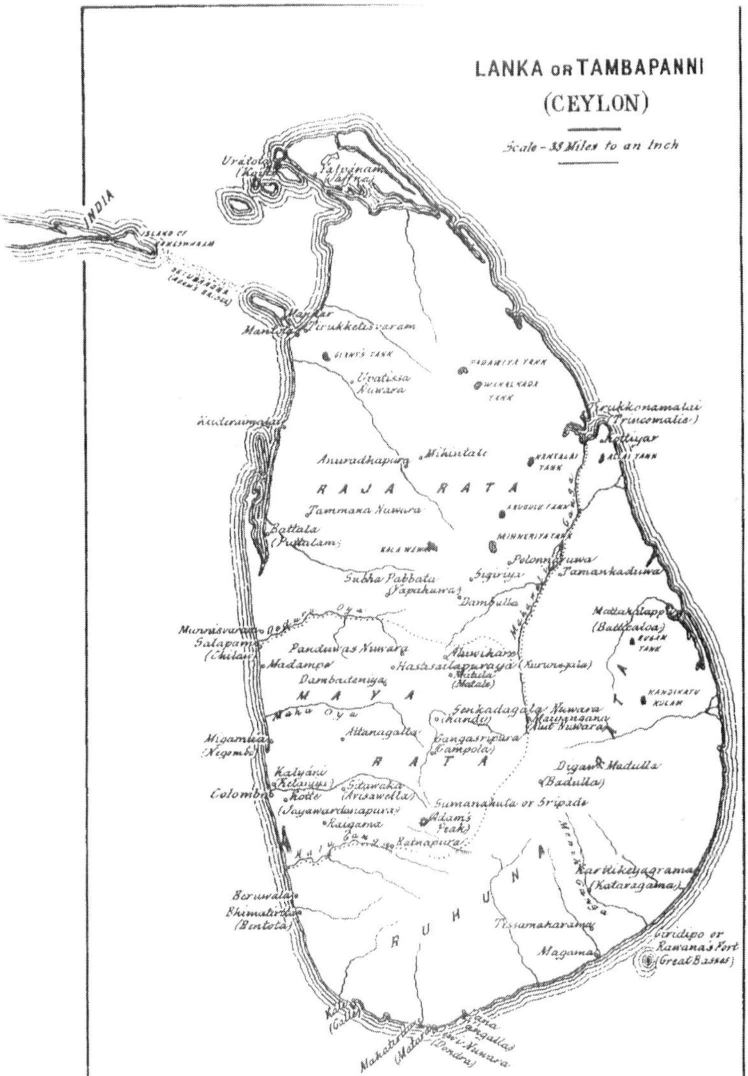

Lith: S. G. O. Colombo No. 71/36.

calls itself by the title of *pillai*, her children, for so she deigned to call them when granting the boon. The Tamil name of the grain (*arisi*) was adopted into the Greek language as ὄρυζα, and through the Latin *oryza* has passed into modern European languages (French *riz*, English *rice*, &c.)

Tamil colonies of agriculturists and artificers were imported in large numbers, and rice and other cultivation introduced. Irrigation works were constructed. In order to secure the organized and continuous labour necessary for their maintenance, the patriarchal village system, which still remains in a modified form, under the name *Gansabháwa*, was introduced. Large military forces were subsidized, and the highest offices of State thrown open to the new allies. The civil and military administration of the Island thus organized and her resources developed, Ceylon rose gradually to a high state of prosperity and civilization. The Island was divided into three great *ratas* or regions; the *Pihiti* or *Raja rata*, so called from its containing the established (*pihiti*) seats of royalty (*raja*), and comprising the whole region to the north of the Mahaweliganga; the *Rohana rata*, bounded on the east and south by the sea and on the north and west by the Mahaweliganga and Kaluganga, and including the mountain zone to which the land rose from the seacoast like a ladder (*rohana*); and the *Máya rata* between the Deduru Oya and Kaluganga, the western sea and the mountain ranges and the Mahaweliganga on the east.

Throughout the twentyfour centuries of native rule rice-cultivation was the principal concern of king and people and amongst the noblest of callings. Kings themselves drove the plough. To build tanks and construct water-courses were regarded as the wisest and most beneficent acts of a good ruler. The extensive ruins scattered in profusion in the ancient kingdoms attest the bounteous care of the kings and the lavish expenditure of money and labour on the national industry, and the names of these kings live in the grateful recollection of the people as benefactors of their race and country.

Great as these irrigation works were, the greatest perhaps in the world, they did not altogether prevent famine in times of severe drought. The native chronicles report the singular manner in which a Sinhalese sovereign (Siri Sangabodhi Raja, *circa* 252 A.D.,) on one such occasion manifested his sympathy with his suffering people. "Having learned that the people were suffering from the effects of a drought, this benevolent king, throwing himself down on the ground in the square of the Mahathupa, pronounced this vow: 'Though I lose my life, I will not rise from this spot until rain shall have fallen sufficient to raise me on its flood from the earth.' Accordingly the ruler of the land remained prostrate on the ground, and the rain cloud instantly poured down his showers. Throughout the island the earth was deluged. But even then he would not rise, as he was not completely buoyed up on the surface of the water. So the officers of the household blocked the drains of the square. Thereupon being lifted by the water, the righteous king rose. In this manner did this all-compassionate sovereign dispel the horrors of the drought." (*Maháwansa*, I., p. 146.)

About 437 B.C., the capital of Ceylon was transferred by king Pandukabhaya, fifth in Wijaya's line, to Anuradhapura, the *Anurogrammum* of Ptolemy, originally founded by one of Wijaya's followers. The city organization was fairly complete and gives proof of no mean administrative capacity as well as advance in sanitary science. The king appointed his uncle "Nagaraguttika," the Mayor of the city. "From that time there have been," says the *Mahâwansa*, "Nagaraguttikas in the capital." Anuradhapura may thus claim to have been among the oldest Municipal corporations in the world. A great marsh was deepened and converted into a tank called Jaya. Friendly relations were established with the aboriginal Yakkhas and their chiefs were given important offices. "He formed the four suburbs of the city and the Abhaya tanks and to the west-ward of the place the great cemetery, and the place of execution and punishment. He employed a body of five hundred *chandalas* (out-castes) to be scavengers of the city and two hundred *chandalas* to be night-men, one hundred and fifty *chandalas* to be carriers of corpses, and the same number of *chandalas* at the cemetery. He formed a village for them on the north-west of the cemetery, and they constantly performed every work according to the directions of the king. To the north-east of this village he established a village of *Nicha chandalas* to serve as cemetery-men to the out-castes. To the northward of that cemetery and between it and the Pásána mountain, a range of buildings was at the same time constructed for the king's huntsmen. To the north-ward of these he formed the Gamini tank. He also constructed a dwelling for the various class of devotees. To the east-ward the king built a residence for the Brahman Jotiya, the Chief Engineer. In the same quarter a Nigantha devotee, named Giri, and many Pasandaka devotees dwelt, and the king built a temple for the Nighanta Kumbandha which was called by his name. To the west-ward of that temple and the east-ward of the huntsmen's buildings, he provided a residence for 500 persons of various foreign religions and faiths." (*Maháwansa*, I., p. 43.)

V.

While Wijaya and his immediate successors were thus improving and developing the Island, on the continent of India the seeds sown by one of the greatest of her sons, Gautama Buddha, about the time that Wijaya left India for Ceylon, were beginning to bear fruit. Buddhism, ousting Brahminism from its pre-eminence, became the prevailing religion under the great emperor Asoka (*circa* 320 B.C.) He has been called the Constantine of Buddhism, an Alexander with Buddhism for his Hellas, a Napoleon with *mettam*, all-embracing love, instead of *gloire* for his guiding light. His grand-father was Chandragupta, the Sandracottus of the Greek historians, at whose court Megasthenes represented king Seleucus, general of Alexander the Great and afterwards successor to his Bactrian and Indian dominions. Inscribed rocks and stone pillars, still found from Cashmere to Orissa, bear testimony to the extent of Asoka's empire, the righteousness and wisdom of his rule, and the nobility of his character.

His active benevolence was not limited to the confines of his empire or to human beings. One of his famous rock edicts records the system of medical aid which he established throughout his dominions and adjoining countries, Ceylon being specially named. "Everywhere within the conquered province of the Raja Piyadasi (Asoka), the beloved of the gods, as well as in the parts occupied by the faithful, such as Chola, Pida, Satyaputra and Ketalaputra, even as far as *Tambapanni* (Ceylon), and moreover within the dominions of Antiochus the Greek, everywhere the heaven-beloved king's double system of medical aid is established, both medical aid for men and medical aid for animals, together with the medicaments of all sorts suitable for men and for animals. And where-ever there is not (such provision), in all such places they shall be prepared and planted, both root-drugs and herbs. And in the public highways wells shall be dug and trees planted for the accommodation of men and animals."

A second inscription appoints officers to watch over domestic life and public morality and to promote instruction among the women as well as the youth.

The essence of religion is declared to consist in reverence to father and mother and spiritual teacher, kindness to servants and dependents, to the aged, to the orphan and destitute, and to Brahmins and Sramans (Buddhist monks), and tenderness to all living creatures; "and this is the true religious devotion, this the sum of religious instruction, viz., that it shall increase the mercy and charity, the truth and purity, the kindness and honesty of the world."

Another inscription records how he sent forth missionaries "to the utmost limits of the barbarian countries" for the spread of the religion of Buddha, and directs the missionaries to mix equally with soldiers, Brahmins and beggars, with the dreaded and the despised, both within the kingdom and in foreign countries, teaching better things. But conversion is to be effected by persuasion, not by the sword. Tolerance is inculcated on the ground that "all faiths aim at moral restraint and purity of life, although all cannot be equally successful in attaining to it." "A man must honor his own faith without blaming that of his neighbour, and thus will but little that is wrong occur. There are even circumstances under which the faith of others should be honoured, and in acting thus a man increases his own faith and weakens that of others. He who acts differently, diminishes his own faith and injures that of another." "Buddhism," as Sir W. Hunter observes, "was at once the most intensely missionary religion in the world and the most tolerant. The character of a proselytizing faith which wins its victories by peaceful means, so strongly impressed upon it by Asoka, has remained a prominent feature of Buddhism to the present day."

By other edicts Asoka prohibits the slaughter of animals for food or sacrifice, he orders a quinquennial humiliation of the people and a republication of the great moral precepts of the Buddhistic creed; he inculcates the true happiness to be found in virtue and that the imparting of virtue is the greatest of all charitable gifts; he contrasts the vain and transitory glory of this world with the reward for which he strives and looks beyond.

No sovereign in history save perhaps Marcus Aurelius, the Stoic philosopher, who shed lustre on the throne of the Cæsars five hundred years later, was animated by so high an ideal of kingly duty. Asoka also collected the body of Buddhistic doctrine into an authoritative version in the Magadhi or Pali language of his central kingdom, a version which for over 2,000 years has formed the Canon of the Southern, including Ceylon, Buddhists.

At the beginning of the third century before Christ, the reigning king of Ceylon, the saintly Tissa, "beloved of the gods," Devánámpiyatissa, became a convert to Buddhism. At his request the Emperor Asoka sent his son Mahinda (307 B.C.) to Ceylon to preach the faith, and later his daughter Sanghamitta as a missionary to the women of Ceylon. By the zeal and eloquence of this noble pair of missionaries Buddhism became established in the Island.

The consummation of that achievement was the arrival (288 B.C.) of a branch of the sacred Bo-tree (*Ficus religiosa*), under the shade of which Gautama Buddha had attained wisdom. The branch, planted with great pomp and ceremony at Anuradhapura, still flourishes there, the oldest historical tree in the world, and the object of profound veneration to millions of Buddhists throughout the world. To this tree, the symbol of Buddha's noble life and teaching, Anuradhapura through all its vicissitudes of centuries owes its escape from the oblivion which has overtaken other mighty cities and kingdoms. So true is it, as Goethe has said, that—

> "Ein geistreich aufgeschlossenes Wort
> Wirkt auf die Ewigkeit."

Perhaps under a renewed impulse of the same spiritual force Anuradhapura may again witness a revival of her ancient splendour.

Eight miles from Anuradhapura, by a road which is the *Via Sacra* of the Buddhist world, stands the Mihintale mountain, revered as the scene of the first interview between the saint Mahinda and his royal convert. A noble flight of steps, more than a thousand in number, leads from the base to the highest peak which is crowned by the Ambasthala dagoba, which enshrines the saint's ashes and commands a view of majestic grandeur. Near by are rock buildings which served as retreats for the monks. Inscriptions, still legible, tell us somewhat of their mode of life. None who destroyed life were permitted to live near the mountain; special offices were allotted various servants and workmen; accounts were to be strictly kept and examined at an assembly of priests; certain allowances of money to every person engaged in the temple service were made for the purchase of flowers, so that none might appear without an offering; cells are assigned to the readers, expounders and preachers; hours of rising, of meditation and ablution are prescribed; careful attention to food and diet for the sick is enjoined; there are instructions to servants of every kind, warders, receivers of revenue, clerks, watchmen, physicians, surgeons, laundry men and others. The minuteness of detail gives an excellent idea of the completeness of arrangement for the orderly and beautiful keeping of the venerated place.

VI.

In the year 237 B.C., the troubles of the Wijaya dynasty began. Two Tamil chiefs in the employ of the king killed him and usurped his throne, which they jointly occupied for twenty-two years, when they were dethroned and slain and the original dynasty was restored.

The Tamils re-established themselves ten years later under Elala, a prince of the Chola dynasty. The dethroned dynasty took refuge in Magampattu, on the southern coast, where the great tank and dagoba at Tissamaharama still stand as monuments of their rule. Elala at Anuradhapura, according to the Buddhist chronicles, though a heretic, "ruled the kingdom for forty-four years, administering justice impartially to friend and foe." At the gate of his palace hung, according to the custom of the Chola kings, the *Arachchi Mani* or "bell of inquiry," communicating with the head of his bed and the ringing of which secured immediate inquiry and redress of grievances. Fables, which the *Mahâwansa* gravely records, grew up that the very birds and beasts sought and obtained redress. His unswerving justice inflicted capital punishment on his son. For an unintentional damage caused to a Buddhist dagoba by his chariot he offered his own life as atonement, but the aggrieved persons were pleased to accept other restitution.

The tomb, erected where he fell by his generous foe Dutugemunu, a scion of the old line, is still regarded with veneration by the Sinhalese. "On reaching the quarter of the city on which it stands," says the chronicle, "it has been the custom for the monarchs of Lanka to silence their music, whatever procession they may be heading." Well may the Sinhalese be proud of chivalry so rare and unprecedented. So uniformly was this homage continued, says Tennent, that so lately as 1818, on the suppression of an attempted rebellion against the British Government, when the defeated aspirant to the throne was making his escape by Anuradhapura, he alighted from his litter on approaching the quarter in which the monument was known to exist, and although weary and almost incapable of exertion, not knowing the precise spot, he continued on foot till assured that he had passed far beyond the ancient memorial.

THUPÁRÀMA DAGOBA, AND ANCIENT PILLARS, AT ANURADHAPURA.

King Dutugemunu in the epics of Buddhism enjoys a renown second only to that of Devanampiyatissa. He commemorated his triumph by numerous magnificent buildings dedicated to religion and charity. Of his nine-storeyed monastery, the Brazen Palace, resting on 1,600 monolithic columns and roofed with plates of brass, a forest of pillars still stands. The ruins of the Ruwanweli and Miriswetiya Dagobas match in greatness and sanctity those of the Tuparama constructed by Devanampiyatissa to enshrine the collar-bone of Buddha. Nor did Dutugemunu forget his patron-god Kartikeya of Kataragama, who had sent him forth to do battle with Elala. His gratitude raised noble structures over the ancient shrine and gifted it with rich endowments.

After Dutugemunu's time the Tamils proved a never-failing source of harassment. They made frequent incursions into Ceylon, and Tamil kings often sat on Wijaya's throne. Walagam Bahu I. (*circa* 104 B.C.) after a short reign lost his kingdom, his queen and the most precious treasure in Ceylon, Buddha's begging-bowl. After 15 years of exile he recovered the two former and in commemoration of his success built the Abhayagiri Dagoba, the most stupendous of this class of structures, rising originally to a height of 405 feet and its ruins after a lapse of 2,000 years standing over 240 feet.

Sometimes the tide of invasion was rolled back into South India, as by king Gaja Bahu, who (113 A.D.) brought back a multitude of captives that the Tamil king had taken, and also a large number of Tamil captives, whom he settled in Alutkuru korale of the Colombo District, Harispattu and Tumpane of the Kandy District and in parts of the Kurunegala District.

Gaja Bahu's triumph is commemorated by a yearly *perahera* festival which is now continued by the Dalada Maligawa at Kandy. But the tooth-relic of Buddha which now heads the procession formed no part of it till about 150 years ago.* At this festival a high place has always been held by the goddess Pattini whose worship was introduced by Gaja Bahu, as recorded in the Tamil classic, *Chilappatikáram*, the work of a contemporary poet. Gaja Bahu brought from India the golden *halamba* or anklet of the goddess, copies of which are the symbols of her worship, and oaths are not infrequently taken on them in courts of justice. No oath is more dreaded by the Sinhalese peasant.

Gaja Bahu also established in honour of the goddess the great national game of *Ankeliya* or horn-pulling, held especially on the occasion of epidemics and conducted on a magnificent scale in the presence of thousands of spectators. It concludes with a torch-light procession through the infected villages, recalling the "need-fires" lighted by farmers in England on the occasion of epidemics among cattle. Many a Sinhalese family traces a hereditary connexion with one or other of the rival factions which in times past celebrated this festival with boisterous merriment and not infrequently with such riotous excess that the kings had to forbid the celebration.

VII.

In the long line of Ceylon kings none perhaps is so revered as Siri Sanghabodhi of whose sympathy and love for his people I have already given a striking illustration. His death was not unworthy of his life. Renouncing his sovereignty to retire into the woods for religious contemplation, he was pursued by the fears of his rival who set a price on his head. When many had died through being mistaken for him, a poor man eager for the reward went in search of the exile,

* This was by order of King Kirti Sri Raja Sinha (1747-1780 A.D.) who did much to revive Buddhism and restored the almost extinct order of monks by importation from Siam.

and accidentally meeting him at Attanagalla but not knowing his identity, mentioned his errand. Siri Sanghabodhi out of compassion for his poverty and for the many that had died, disclosed himself and severed his own head. This supreme act of self-sacrifice earned for him from his remorse-stricken rival the erection of the celebrated Attanagalla Vihara (not far from Veyangoda and still a venerated shrine) and the still higher glory that great Sinhalese kings thenceforward assumed *Siri Sanghabodhi* as one of their principal titles.

In Siri Sanghabodhi (whom the modern world would perhaps regard as weak and superstitious) the people recognised a sovereign who most realized Buddha's ideals of self-conquest and universal charity, of humility and self-sacrifice, which the Master preached in many a sermon and illustrated in many a dialogue and story, and not least in that beautiful and popular collection known as the *Játaka* or birth-stories. Here, e.g., is one known as "the Banyan deer birth-story." A lady, the mother of Kumára Kássapa, had been unjustly found guilty of immoral conduct and was declared innocent through the intervention of the Master. Then it is said that the brethren talking this matter over at even-tide, the Master came there, and learning the subject of their discourse, said: "Not only has the Tathágata [Buddha] proved a support and protection to these two [the lady and her son]; formerly also he was the same." Then, on request, he revealed that matter, concealed by change of birth.

Once upon a time when king Brahmadatta was reigning in Benares, the Bodhisatta was reborn as a deer, a king of the deer, by name the Banyan Deer. The herd of the Banyan Deer was shut in the king's park, as also another herd of the Branch Deer. The king of men or his cook went daily to hunt for deer for venison. For each one killed many were wounded or harassed by the chase. So the golden-coloured

Banyan Deer went to the king Branch Deer and persuaded him to a compact that lots should be cast and that every day the one deer on whom the lot fell should go voluntarily to the cook's place of execution and lay his head upon the block. And this was done. And so by the daily death of one the rest were saved from torture and distress. Now one day the lot fell upon a pregnant doe in the Branch Deer's herd. She applied to the king of the herd to order that the lot, "which was not meant to fall on two at once," should pass her by. But he harshly bade her begone to the block. Then she went to king Banyan Deer and told her piteous tale. He said he would see to it, and he went himself and laid his head on the block.

Now the king of men had decreed immunity to the kings of the two herds. When the cook saw king Banyan Deer lying there with his head on the block, he ran and told the king of men, who mounted his chariot and with his retinue hurried to the spot, and said: "My friend, king Banyan Deer, did I not grant your life? Why are you here?" Then the king of the deer told him all. And the king of men was greatly touched, and said: "Rise up. I grant you your lives, both to you and to her." Then the rejoinder came: "But though two be thus safe, what shall the rest of the herds do, O king of men?" So they also obtained security. And when the Banyan Deer had likewise procured protection for all the various sorts of living things, he exhorted the king of men to justice and mercy, preaching the truth to him "with the grace of a Buddha."

And the doe gave birth to a son beautiful as buds of flowers, and he went playing with the Branch Deer's herd. Then his mother exhorted him:—

> "Follow rather the Banyan Deer;
> Cultivate not the Branch!
> Death, with the Banyan, were better far
> Than, with the Branch, long life."

And the Banyan Deer made a compact with the men that wherever leaves were tied round a field, the deer should not trespass, and he made all the deer keep to the bargain. From that time, they say, the sign of the tying of leaves was seen in the fields.

Then the Master identified the characters. "He who was then the Branch Deer is now Devadatta [a schismatic], his herd the members of the order who followed him in his schism, the doe is now Kumára Kássapa's mother, the deer she gave birth to is now her son Kumára Kássapa, the king of the men is Ananda [Buddha's favourite disciple], and Banyan, the king of the deer, was I myself."

VIII.

The Buddhist scriptures, known as the *Tripiṭaka* or the Three Baskets or Collections, were, 88 B.C., reduced to writing and so protected from the corruptions and errors inseparable from oral tradition. This was done at the romantic cave-temple of Alu Vihara in the Matale District by 500 learned and saintly monks assembled by order of Walagam Bahu I. This did not, however, prevent the growth of schism which even in his time had manifested itself, having its headquarters in the Abhayagiri Vihara which he founded and which set itself up against the ancient seat of orthodoxy, the Maha Vihara. The dissensions increased as time went on.

From the beginning of the 3rd century A.D. the Buddhist church was distracted by a heresy called the Wytulian. Of its nature little is known, but it was deemed sufficiently grave to call forth extreme measures of persecution from the Sinhalese kings, hitherto so tolerant. The heresy, however, time after time reasserted itself till about 275 A.D. it even found a champion in the king Maha Sen. He dispossessed the orthodox monks, overthrew their great monastery the Brazen Palace, and with its materials constructed buildings for the heretics. A popular revolt compelled him to retrace his steps and to make ample amends. He restored the buildings he had destroyed, erected new monasteries and nunneries, constructed the stately Jetawanarama Dagoba and numerous tanks, including the vast lakes of Mineri and Kantalai, and made gifts without limit to the orthodox monks. A grateful people have awarded him divine honors and worship him as an incarnation of the Kataragama god under the name Minneri Sami. On his death (301 A.D.) ended the Great Line or Mahawansa, and the Little Line or Suluwansa began, in the veins of whose sovereigns no longer ran (according to the Chronicles) the pure blood of the Solar dynasty.

To this line, however, belonged many illustrious kings, among whom were the painter and sculptor-king Jeṭṭha Tissa (330 A.D.) and the great surgeon Buddhadasa (339 A.D.). The Sinhalese kings from the earliest times, mindful of the health of their subjects, maintained systems of medical aid, following in the footsteps of their great exemplar, the Indian Emperor Asoka. King Dutugemunu (200 B.C.) on his death-bed relates among his meritorious acts: "I have daily maintained at 18 different places hospitals provided with suitable diet and medicines prepared by medical practitioners for the infirm" (*Maháwansa*, I. p. 125). A rock inscription at Mihintale (*circ.* 362 A.D.) records that a physician and surgeon were borne on the establishment of great monasteries. King Buddhadasa is said "to have entertained for mankind at large the compassion a parent feels for his children. He rendered happy the indigent by distribution of riches, protected the rich in their property and life, patronized the virtuous, discountenanced the wicked, and comforted the diseased by providing medical relief," (Ibid p. 155). He composed a great work, still extant, on surgery, called *Saraththasangaha*. He

KINGS OF THE MAHAVANSA OR GREAT DYNASTY. (B.C. 543—A.D. 304).

No.	Name.	Date of Accession.	Capital.	Length of Reign.*
		B.C.		
1	Vijaya I.	543	Tammanna Nuwara	38
2	Upatissa (*Regent*)	505	Upatissa Nuwara	1
3	Panduvasdev	504	,,	30
4	Abhaya	474	,,	20
	(*Interregnum of* 17 *years*)	454—437		17
5	Pandukābhaya	437	Anuradhapura	70†
6	Mutasiva	367	,,	60†
7	Dēvānampiya Tissa	307	,,	40
8	Uttiya	267	,,	10
9	Mahāsiva	257	,,	10
10	Suratissa	247	,,	10
11	Sena and Guttika (Tamils)	237	,,	22
12	Asela	215	,,	10
13	Elāra (Tamil)	205	,,	44
14	Dutugemunu	161	,,	24
15	Sadātissa	137	,,	18
16	Tuluna *or* Tullatthana	119	,,	$1\frac{1}{3}$ mths.
17	Ladetissa	119	,,	$9\frac{2}{3}$
18	Kalunna	109	,,	6
19	Valagambāhu	104	,,	5 mths.
20	*Five Tamil Kings*			
	Pulahattha	103	,,	15
	Bayiha	100	,,	
	Panayamāia	98	,,	
	Pelaiyamāra	91	,,	
	Dāthiya	90	,,	
	Valagambāhu (*restored*)	88	,,	12
21	Mahasilu Mahatis	76	,,	14
22	Coranāga	62	,,	12
23	Kudā Tissa	50	,,	3
24	Anulā (*Queen*)	47	,,	5
25	Makalan Tissa	42	,,	22
26	Bhātikabhaya	20	,,	28
		A.D.		
27	Mahadeliyā	9	,,	12
28	Adagemunu	21	,,	$8\frac{3}{4}$
29	Kanijānu Tissa	30	,,	3
30	Chūlābhaya	33	,,	1
31	Sivali (*Queen*)	35	,,	4 mths.
	(*Interregnum of* 3 *years*)	35—38	,,	3
32	Ilanāga	38	,,	6
33	Sandamuhunu	44	,,	$8\frac{1}{2}$
34	Yasalālaka Tissa	52	,,	$7\frac{2}{3}$
35	Subha	60	,,	6
36	Vasabha	66	,,	44
37	Vankanāsika Tissa	110	,,	3
38	Gajabāhu I.	113	,,	22
39	Mahalunā	135	,,	6
40	Bahatiya II.	141	,,	24
41	Kanitu Tissa	165	,,	28
42	Sulunā *or* Chūlanāga	193	,,	2
43	Kuddanāga	195	,,	1
44	Sirināga I.	196	,,	19
45	Voharaka Tissa	215	,,	22
46	Abhayanāga	237	,,	8
47	Sirināga II.	245	,,	2
48	Vijaya II. (or Vijayindu)	247	,,	1
49	Sangatissa I.	248	,,	4
50	Siri Sangabō I.	252	,,	2
51	Gothābhaya	254	,,	13
52	Detutis I., *or* Jetthatissa	267	,,	10
53	Mahasen	277 to 304	,,	27

* In *years*, unless otherwise stated.

† These reigns have probably been extended by the historians in order to put back the arrival of Vijaya in Ceylon and the commencement of his reign to 543, the traditional date of Buddha's death.

extended the benefit of his surgical skill to the lowest castes and even animals. He provided hospitals and medical practitioners in all villages, and on the main roads asylums for the crippled, deformed and destitute.

This policy was continued by the great Parakrama Bahu (1150 A.D.) of whom the *Mahawansa* records (II. 194-5): "And this ruler of men built further a large hall that could contain many hundreds of sick persons, and provided it also with all things that were needful, as stated underneath. To every sick person he allowed a male and a female servant, that they might minister to him by day and by night, and furnish him with the physic that was necessary and with divers kinds of food. And many store houses also did he build therein, filled with grain and other things, and with all things that were needful for medicine. And he also made provision for the maintenance of wise and learned physicians who were versed in all knowledge and skilled in searching out the nature of diseases. And he took care to discern the different wants of the sick, and caused the physicians to minister to them, as seemed necessary, both by day and night. And it was his custom, on the four Uposatha days (quarter-days of the moon) of every month, to cast off his royal robes and, after that he had solemnly undertaken to observe the precepts, to purify himself and put on a clean garment, and visit that hall together with his ministers. And, being endued with a heart full of kindness, he would look at the sick with an eye of pity, and, being eminent in wisdom and skilled in the art of healing, he would call before him the physicians that were employed there and inquire fully of the manner of their treatment. And if so be that it happened that the treatment that they had pursued was wrong, the king, who was the best of teachers, would point out wherein they had erred, and, giving reasons therefor, would make clear to them the course that they should have pursued according to science; also to some sick persons he would give physic with his own hands. Likewise also he would inquire of the health of all those that were sick, and unto such as were cured of their diseases he would order raiment to be given. And as he desired greatly to gain merit, he would partake of merit at the hands of the physicians, and impart his own merit to them, and then return to his own palace. In this manner, indeed, did this merciful king, free from disease himself, cure the sick of their divers diseases from year to year."

IX.

In the beginning of the 5th century A.D. two notable visitors arrived in the Island. The only commentaries on the *Tripiṭaka* existed in Ceylon. In search of them came to Anuradhapura, about 400 A.D., the learned Brahmin Buddhaghosa, "the Voice of Buddha," from Northern India. He gave a decided impetus to Buddhist learning by translating the Sinhalese commentaries (*Aṭṭhakathá*) into Pali and composing others, and his works are regarded as absolute authorities in the interpretation of the Buddhist scriptures. He may be regarded as the second founder of Buddhism in Ceylon.*

About 412 A.D., the Chinese monk-traveller Fa-Hian landed in Ceylon, with which his countrymen had for centuries maintained continuous commercial and religious intercourse. He visited Anuradhapura, then in its glory, and remained there two years engaged in transcribing the sacred books. He has vividly described† the splendour and magnificence of Anuradhapura and of the national religion and the prosperity of the Island. Two hundred years later,

* Maháwansa, I. p. 159.

† Beal's *Buddhist Records of the Western World* Vol. I., pp. *LXXII.*, et seq.

KINGS OF THE SULUVANSA OR LOWER DYNASTY FROM 304 to 1037 A.D.

No.	Name.	Date of Accession.	Capital.	Length of Reign.*
		A.D.		
54	Kirti Siri Meghavarna, or Sirimevan	304	Anuradhapura ...	28
55	Jettha Tissa or Detutis II.	332	,, ...	9
56	Buddhadāsa	341	,, ...	29
57	Upatissa II.	370	,, ...	42
58	Mahānāma	412	,, ...	22
59	Sotth' Sena	434	,, ...	1 day
60	Chattagāhaka... ...	434	,, ...	1
61	Mitta Sena	435	,, ...	1
62	*Six Tamil Kings*			
	Pandu	436	,, ...	25
	Parinda	441	,, ...	
	Khudda Parinda ...	444	,, ...	
	Tiritara	460	,, ...	
	Dathiya	460	,, ...	
	Pithiya	463	,, ...	
63	Dhātu Sena	461	,, ...	18
64	Kāsyapa I.	479	,, & Sigiriya	18
65	Mugalan I.	497	Anuradhapura ...	18
66	Kumāradāsa or Dhatusēna	515	,, ...	9
67	Kirti Sena	524	,, ...	9 mths.
68	Siva	524	,, ...	25 days
69	Upatissa III.	525	,, ...	1½
70	Silākāla	526	,, ...	13
71	Dapulu Sen I. ...	539	,, ...	6 mths.
72	Mugalan II.	540	,, ...	20
73	Kirti Sri Meghavarna ...	560	,, ...	19 days
74	Mahānāga	561	,, ...	3
75	Agrabōdhi I.	564	,, ...	34
76	Agrabōdhi II.... ...	598	,, ...	10
77	Sanghatissa II. ...	608	,, ..	2 mths.
78	Dala Mugalan ...	608	,, ...	6
79	Asigrāhaka or Silumeguvanna	614	,, ...	9
80	Agrabōdhi III. (or Siri Sangabō II.)	623	,, ...	6 mths.
81	Jetta Tissa or Detutis III,	623	,, ...	6 mths.
80	Agrabōdhi III. (*restored*) ...	624	,, ...	16
82	Dāthōpatissa I. ...	640	,, ...	12
83	Kāsyapa II.	652	,, ...	9
84	Dappula I.	661	,, & Ruhuna	3
85	Dāthōpatissa II. (Hattha Datha I.)	664	Anuradhapura ..	9
86	Agrabōdhi IV. or Siri Sangabō III.	673	,, ...	16
87	Datta	689	,, ...	2
88	Hattha Dātha II. or Hunannaru Riyandala ...	691	,, ...	6 mths.
89	Mānavamma or Mahalēpāna	691	,, ...	35
90	Agrabōdhi V.	726	,, ...	6
91	Kasyapa III.	732	,, ...	6
92	Mahinda I.	738	,, ...	3
93	Akbō Salamevan or Agrabōdhi VI.	741	,, ...	40
94	Agrabōdhi VII. ...	781	Polonnaruwa ...	6
95	Mahinda II.	787	Anuradhapura ...	20
96	Dappula II.	807	,, ...	5
97	Mahinda III.	812	,, ...	4
98	Agbō or Agrabōdhi VIII. ...	816	,, ...	11
99	Dappula III.	827	Beramini-paya ...	16
100	Agrabōdhi IX.... ...	843	Anuradhapura ...	3
101	Sena I. (Sila Megha) ...	846	Polonnaruwa ...	20
102	Sena II.	866	,, ...	35
103	Udaya I.	901	,, ...	11
104	Kasyapa IV.	912	,, ...	17
105	Kasyapa V.	929	,, ...	10
106	Dappula IV.	939	,, ...	7 mths.
107	Dappula V.	940	,, ...	12
108	Udaya II.	952	,, ...	3
109	Sena III.	955	,, ...	9
110	Udaya III.	964	,, ...	8
111	Sena IV.	972	,, ...	3
112	Mahinda IV.	975	,, ...	16
113	Sena V.	991	,, ...	10
114	Mahinda V.	1001	Anuradhapura ...	36

* In years, unless otherwise stated.

when another Chinese traveller, Hiouen-Thsang, visited India, he met numbers of exiles from Ceylon, who informed him that they had fled from civil commotions in the Island, in which the religion had undergone persecution, the king had lost his life, cultivation had been interrupted, and the Island exhausted by famine.

In the reign of king Dhatusena (461-479 A.D.) the great chronicle of the *Mahâwansa* was composed by his uncle, the monk Mahanama, from annals and traditions then extant. In the two chief monasteries in Anuradhapura, the Great Minster and the North Minster, the canonical books had been handed down from generation to generation in Pali, with commentaries upon them, in Sinhalese, interspersed with mnemonic verses in Pali. In the third century A.D. some one collected such of the Pali verses as referred to the history of Ceylon, piecing them together by other verses to make a consecutive narrative. The poem thus constructed was called the *Dipavansa*, the *Island Chronicle*. Shortly afterwards the celebrated Buddhaghosa, arriving from India, rewrote in Pali the Sinhalese commentaries which are now lost. In his work, which has supplanted them, we may trace the ancient tradition. He quotes from the old Sinhalese commentary a number of mnemonic verses also contained in the *Dipavansa* and gives in Pali the substance of the Sinhalese prose with which they had been originally accompanied. On the basis of these works and of popular legends, Mahanama, a literary artist, who lived a generation after Buddhaghosa, wrote the *Mahâwansa*, which is really an epic poem of remarkable merit, with the national idol, Dutugemunu, the conqueror of the invading hosts of the Tamils, as his hero. What he says of other kings, and of Asoka amongst them, is only by way of introduction or of epilogue to the main story.

It is written in Pali verse and covers the period B.C. 543 to A.D. 301. It was continued by order of

Parakrama Bahu II. of Dambadeniya up to about 1262 A.D. by the monk Dharmakirti, and again to about 1295 in the reign of Pandita Parakrama Bahu IV. of Kurunegala, and lastly to 1758 by the monk Tibbotuwawa by order of king Kirtisri. It may be said of the writers of these chronicles, as Hume said of the old English chroniclers: "The monks who lived remote from public affairs, considered the civil transactions as subservient to the ecclesiastical and were strongly affected with credulity, with the love of wonder, and with a propensity to imposture." The last remark perhaps does injustice to these simple Buddhist monks who seem to have fully believed what they wrote and from whom it would be unreasonable to expect that sort of historical training which is of quite recent growth even in Europe.

The translation made of the *Mahdwansa* by George Turnour of the Ceylon Civil Service and published in 1837, constitutes a great landmark in Oriental archæology and history. From him invaluable help was derived by James Prinsep who was then wearing himself out in his enthusiastic efforts to decipher the coins and inscriptions of India, while the very alphabets and dialects were as yet uncertain. Without the help of Turnour's *Mahdwansa** the striking identification of king Piyadasi of the inscriptions with the king Asoka of history would never have been made, and ancient Indian history would still be in a maze.

Excavations by General Cunningham in the *Topes* (brick burial-mounds) of Sanchi in Central India have furnished striking and unexpected confirmation of the *Mahdwansa*. In a curt record (ch. 12) the chronicler gives the names of the missionaries sent out by Tissa,

* Turnour's translation covered the first 38 chapters and was published in 1837. He had previously in 1832 published in the Ceylon Almanac an Epitome of Ceylon History, which is reprinted as Appendix to Forbes' '*Eleven Years in Ceylon*,' *1833*.

ROCK-FORT OF SIGIRIYA.

son of Moggali, the President of the third Convocation held by Asoka. They were sent to Kashmir, to Kandahar, to the Himalaya, to the border lands on the Indus, to Burma, to South India and Ceylon. Each party consisted of a leader and four assistants. Of the five missionaries to the Himalayan region three are named as Majjhima, Kassapagotta, and Dundubhissara. Now General Cunningham found buried at Sanchi funeral-urns containing ashes of the distinguished persons in whose honour the *Topes* had been built. One of the urns bore an inscription in letters of the 3rd century B.C. with the simple legend: "Of the good man Kassapagotta, the teacher of all the Himalayan region." On another urn is the legend: "Of the good man Majjhima;" on another: "Of the good man, Gotiputta of the Himalaya, successor of Dundubhissara."

King Dhatusena, whose reign is memorable for the composition of the *Mahāwansa*, came to a terrible end. His elder son Kasyapa seized and threw him into a dungeon where he was walled up alive. The monster was driven from the capital by the indignation of the people and established himself on a steep and solitary rock, 30 miles away, where he built himself a fortress which is one of the sights of Ceylon and contains beautiful frescoes which are invaluable as illustrations of the art and the customs of the time. Remorse for his crime gradually crept over him and he sought in vain to expiate it and win peace of mind. "He made many images, almshouses and the like," says the *Mahawansa*, but he lived on in fear of the world to come and of Mugalan." This was his younger brother who had fled to India on the father's murder. In eighteen years he returned with a large army and defeated the parricide who then put an end to his own life. Mugalan re-established the capital at Anuradhapura, converted the Sigiriya fortress into a *vihara* and bestowed it on the monk Mahanama who composed the *Mahāwansa*.

Mugalan's son was the poet-king Kumaradasa. In his court was the poet Kalidasa to whom he was devotedly attached. On one occasion the king, while in a house which he used to visit, wrote on the wall two lines of a verse, adding underneath a promise to reward anyone who completed it. Kalidasa, seeing the inscription, wrote the concluding lines. A woman in the house murdered him and claimed the reward. The king saw through the fraud, as she could not write poetry. Inquiry established the murder of his friend. Overwhelmed with grief, the king threw himself on Kalidasa's funeral pyre and perished in the flames (524 A.D.).

X.

In the sixth century A.D., the first mention occurs in the native chronicles of coconut plantations, destined to form a fruitful source of wealth to future generations. The coco-palm is not indigenous to Ceylon. Its original habitat was the tropical Islands of the Pacific, from which it has extended to the coast of the East and West Indies, Ceylon and tropical America. This wide distribution was favoured by the peculiar triangular shape of the fruit, which, dropping into the sea from trees growing on any shore, would be carried by tides and currents to be cast up and vegetate on distant coasts. In Ceylon the plant first grew on the southern coast, which is the coast most exposed to such currents. King Agrabodhi (*circa* 564 A.D.) is credited by the chronicler with having made a coconut plantation 36 miles in extent in the south of the Island, probably near Weligama, where a Vihara contains a supposed memorial of the king. This policy was continued in the twelfth century by king Parakrama Bahu, who formed a coconut plantation from Bentota to the Kaluganga, and in later times by the Dutch rulers of the Island.

STATUE OF KING PARAKRAMA BAHU AT POLONNARUWA.

TEMPLE OF THE TOOTH, KANDY.

The Tamil influence remained supreme at Anuradhapura from the seventh century till at last in 769 A.D., about the time of the first invasion of Spain by the Saracens, the city was abandoned to the Tamils and the capital transferred to Polonnaruwa, or Pulastya-nagara, the site probably of a pre-historic city named after Pulastya, the grand-father of Ravana, one of the heroes of the *Rámáyana*. Polonnaruwa soon rivalled Anuradhapura in magnificence. But the Tamil inroads continued, and about the time of the Norman Conquest of England the Sinhalese king was taken captive, and Polonnaruwa was made a vice-royalty of the Chola kings of India.

Gradually the Sinhalese rule was re-established at Polonnaruwa. Here in the twelfth century ruled the greatest of the Sinhalese kings, Parakrama Bahu. An adept in all the arts of statesmanship and war, his happy genius followed every track with like success. He re-conquered Ceylon from the Tamils and established peace, so that, as an inscription on the rock at Dambulla records, "even a woman might traverse the Island with a precious jewel and not be asked what it was." He carried his victorious standards into South India, Cambodia, and Siam. Vast ruins still extant, but rarely visited, bear witness to his power and piety. His career, fit theme for an epic poem, is hardly remembered save by the antiquarian. When shall a Sinhalese Valmiki arise to sing the story of Parakrama's glorious life and fix it among the imperishable traditions of the Sinhalese race?

It was not long before Polonnaruwa, too, had to be abandoned to the Tamils, who came now not from the old seats of the Pandya and Chola dynasties, but from Kalinga (Northern Circars). Their domination was marked, if the chronicles are to be believed, by more than ordinary cruelty. "Like the giants of Mára they destroyed the kingdom and the religion of the land. Alas, alas!" "The whole island resembled a dwelling in flames or a house darkened by funeral rites." Cries which recall the wails of the Saxon chronicles of England during the Norman rule at about the same period. "The land was filled with devils and evil men. Never was there more misery and never acted heathens worse than these." [After a recapitulation of their deeds.] "The earth bare no corn, you might as well have tilled the sea, for the land was all ruined by such deeds, and it was said openly that Christ and his Saints slept." The uneasy seat of government in Ceylon had to be shifted from time to time to Dambadeniya, Yapahu, Kurunegala, (all in the Kurunegala District), Gampola, Kotte, Sitawaka, and finally Kandy.

XI.

Among the kings of this later time a high place must be given to Parakrama Bahu II., of Dambadeniya, who was not only, like his great name-sake, a warrior and an administrator, but also a great scholar and, like his father Wijaya Bahu III., a patron of learning.

The latter is reported in the *Rája Ratnákari* to have "established a school in every village and charged the priests who superintended the same to take nothing from the learners, promising that they would be rewarded for their trouble by himself; and thus every day infinite crowds of priests were daily at the king's door; receiving rice and clothing for their trouble of teaching; and to the higher order of priests who did not leave their monasteries, the king ordered their victuals and what they wanted to be sent. He also examined the progress made by the pupils and, according to their merit in learning, promised them that they should be made priests; and the most eminent among them he appointed to particular stations to preach. Having brought religion and learning to this flourishing state, the king exhorted all ranks to persevere in this manner and thus greatly encouraged religion."

In ancient Ceylon, as in Burma to this day, the national instructors were the Buddhist monks, and from the earliest times the kings took a warm interest in education. In an inscription on the Mihintale tablets (Müller's *Ancient Inscriptions of Ceylon* p. 85.) king Mahinda who ruled at Polonnaruwa (*circa.* 1000 A.D.) grants, *inter alia*, a village to a teacher in the Ambasthala temple at Mihintale. Parakrama Bahu VI. who ruled at Kotte (1410-1462 A.D.) was the Mæcenas of his age and was himself a scholar and author. He established and endowed two great educational institutions, one at Totagamuwa, the other at Keragala, the former presided over by Ceylon's greatest poet, Sri Rahula Sthawira, commonly called Totagamuwa.

The former institution was called the *Wijayabahu Pirivena*, and was established at Totagamuwe Vihare, which stands between the 57th and 58th mile-posts on the road from Colombo to Galle. It was a University catholic in its aims, and provided instruction for Buddhists and Hindus, clerical and lay, in all the knowledge of the time. There were classes and lectures in (1) the Buddhist Canon in all its branches (for Buddhist monks), (2) the Sinhalese, Pali, Sanskrit and Tamil languages and literatures, (3) the Four Vedas and the connected literature (for Brahmin students), (4) Astronomy with special study of the *Surya Siddhanta*, (5) Medicine, (6) Prosody, (7) Dramaturgy, (8) Poetry, (Sanskrit, Pali, Sinhalese and Tamil). The Chancellor of the University was Sri Rahula Sthawira, a scholar whose reputation extended over the greater part of Asia. He was master of the Sanskrit, Prakrit, Magadhi, Sauraseni, Apabhransa and Paisachi languages, and therefore had the title of *Sadbhásha paramesvara* (Lord of the six languages.) He himself took part in the lectures. A vivid picture of the University and its throngs of students is given in the *Gira Sandesa*,* a contemporary poem composed in honor of the

* Stanzas 204 et seq.

Chancellor. His literary works—the classic poems *Kavyasekara*, *Selalihini Sandesa* and *Paravi Sandesa*, and the commentary *Panchika Pradipa* on Moggalana's Pali Grammar,—have transmitted his name with undying renown to posterity.

Parakrama Bahu II of Dambadeniya ruled thirty-five years (1240—1275 A.D.) and with the aid of his son Wijaya Bahu whom he appointed Vice-regent, brought all Ceylon under his rule, repelled two successive Malay invasions, restored the ancient capitals of Anuradhapura and Polonnaruwa, and was crowned king at the last-named city.

The *Rájávaliya* relates that in an address to his sons he reminded them that, having conquered the Tamils, he had united under one rule the three kingdoms of the Island, the Pihiti rata of 450,000 villages, Rohana rata of 770,000, and Maya rata of 250,000, or a total of 1,470,000 villages. Taking only a million villages, and allowing two houses to a village and five persons to a house, the population would be ten millions as against a little over three and a half millions at the present day.

This can hardly be deemed an extravagant estimate. As Tennent observes: "The labour necessary to construct one of these gigantic irrigation works" (with the ruins of which the Island is strewn) "is in itself an evidence of local density of population; but their multiplication by successive kings, and the constantly recurring record of district after district brought under cultivation in each successive reign, demonstrate the steady increase of inhabitants and the multitude of husbandmen whose combined and sustained toil was indispensable to keep these prodigious structures in productive activity .... No one who has visited the regions now silent and deserted, once the homes of millions, can hesitate to believe that when the Island was in the zenith of its prosperity, the population of Ceylon must of necessity have been at least ten times as great as it is at the present day."

The decline of population was most probably due to the troublous times of foreign war and internecine strife that preceded the establishment of the British dominion. How rapidly a population may decline was illustrated by Germany during the Thirty Years' War (1618—1648 A.D.). The population fell from twenty to less than ten millions in that period.

At the close of the thirteenth century, according to king Parakrama Bahu's address to his sons, the population was distributed in the three regions in the proportion of 31 per cent. in Pihiti rata, 52 per cent. in Rohana rata, and 17 per cent. in Maya rata. At present the proportion stands, roughly, as 19, 46, and 35. The most striking change is the advance, by over 100 per cent., of the last region, the western sea coast and its vicinity, and the decline by almost as much in the population of the ancient kingdoms, a decline more marked still, if, excluding the Jaffna peninsula, we consider the true "royal" country, the Anuradhapura, Mullaittivu, and Mannar Districts, which, embracing about one-fourth of the total area of the Island, holds less than 3 per cent. of the total population.

The change indicates clearly the difference caused in the condition of the Island by the disorganization of its great irrigation system and the consequent decay of the national industry, rice-cultivation, and by the advent of Europeans. Population and wealth have faded away from their ancient seats and gathered towards the coast The Island, no longer self-sufficient or self-centred, is dependent for its prosperity mainly on foreign enterprise, on the European capitalist and planter, and the South Indian labourer and tradesman. The wealth that trickles from this source, circulating through the country, maintains among the native population an air of prosperity, which will hardly long survive the stopping, by any cause, of the fountain, unless new sources of wealth are created and maintained by indigenous labour and energy.

England in the fourteenth century was, in respect of population and prosperity, hardly better off than Ceylon. A writer in the *Encyclopædia Brittanica* (edition 1902, vol. 26, p. 675) says: "The population of England from the Conquest to the fourteenth century is estimated at between 1½ and 2½ millions. London, it is believed, had a population of about 40,000. Other towns were small. Two or three of the larger had four or five thousand inhabitants. The only substantial building in a village, apart perhaps from the manor-house, was the church, used for many secular as well as religious purposes. In the towns the mud or wood-paved huts sheltered a people who, accepting a common poverty, traded in little more than the necessaries of life. (Green, *Town Life in the Fifteenth Century*, I., 13). The population was stationary. Famine and pestilence were of frequent occurrence (Creighton, *Epidemics in Britain*, p. 19), and for the careless there was waste at harvest time and want in winter. Hunger was the drill sergeant of society." What a change to a population of 32½ millions, a public revenue of 140 millions sterling, and the sovereignty of a world-wide empire! Not by "flying with others' wings" was this high place won. Only by ceaseless energy and the strenuous pursuit of high ideals has England been able to raise herself and "soar triumphant through the lips of men."

XII.

Parakrama Bahu's son and viceroy, Wijaya Bahu, by his deeds of valour, his reconquest of Ceylon, the nobility of his character, and his devotion to his father, was the idol of his people, who bestowed on him the title of *Bosat* which is reserved for those who have nearly attained Buddha-hood. He sat on his father's throne barely two years in his own right, being assassinated by a traitorous general who himself received short shrift from the North Indian warriors in the king's service who placed his brother on the throne.

It was about this time that a princess of Ceylon became the heroine of one of the most stirring tales of Indian history. Her name Padmávati has been transmitted with renown to posterity by tradition and the bards of Rajasthan. She was married to Ratan Sen, the over-lord of the Rajput confederacy and Rana or Sovereign of Chittore, a prince held in reverence throughout India as the lineal descendant of the hero of the *Rámáyana*, and whose modern representative at Udaipur is still accorded the highest place among the chiefs of India. The fame of Padmávati's beauty and accomplishments reached the ears of Alla-ud-din, the Mohammedan Emperor of Delhi who, longing to make her his Empress, invaded Chittore. The Rajputs resisted the imperial arms with their wonted heroism. After a long and fruitless siege Alla-ud-din restricted his desire to a mere sight of this extraordinary beauty reflected through the medium of mirrors. Relying on the faith of the Rajput, he entered Chittore slightly guarded and, having gratified his wish, returned. The Rajput chief, unwilling to be outdone in confidence, accompanied Alla-ud-din to the foot of the fortress, amid many complimentary excuses from his guest at the trouble he thus occasioned. It was for this he had risked his own safety, relying on the superior faith of the Hindu. Here an ambush was ready, and the Hindu king was made prisoner and his liberty made dependent on the surrender of Padmávati.

Despair reigned in Chittore, and it was anxiously debated whether she should be resigned as ransom. She expressed her acquiescence and, having provided the wherewithal to secure herself from dishonour, she devised with two chiefs of her Ceylon clan a scheme in pursuance of which intimation was given to Alla-ud-din that on the day he withdrew from the trenches she would arrive, but in a manner befitting her station, attended by her ladies-in-waiting and by others who would accompany her to Delhi to pay her this last mark of respect, and strict orders were to be issued to prevent the decorum and privacy of the Rajput ladies from being violated by curiosity. 700 covered litters proceeded to the imperial camp, borne by armed soldiers disguised as porters. The imperial tents were enclosed with tapestry, the litters were deposited, and half an hour was granted for a parting interview between the Rana and his bride. They then placed him in a litter and bore him away, leaving the greater number of the supposed damsels behind to accompany the queen to Delhi. Alla-ud-din had no intention to permit the Rana's return and was becoming impatient of the length of the interview, when instead of the Rana and his queen the devoted band issued from their litters. Alla-ud-din was, however, well guarded. Pursuit was ordered, but the Rajputs covered the retreat till they perished to a man. A fleet horse was in reserve for the Rana and carried him safely to the fort, at the gate of which Alla-ud-din's host was encountered by the heroes of Chittore. Animated by enthusiasm for their king and the honour of their queen, they devoted themselves to destruction. Few survived this slaughter of the flower of Rajput chivalry. The havoc made in Alla-ud-din's ranks by their heroism and the dread of their determined resistance obliged him to raise the siege.

Recruiting his strength, he returned to the siege with renewed vigour. The defence had not recovered from the loss of so many brave men, but was maintained with incredible valour. It was in vain. Eleven out of twelve sons of the king fell in succession, leading the fight, and then he called his chiefs around him and said: "Now I devote myself for Chittore." But another awful sacrifice was to precede this act of self-devotion; the terrible rite of *Johur* was to be performed. The funeral pyre was lighted within the great subterranean retreat and the defenders of Chittore saw pass in procession their wives and daughters to the number of several thousands. The fair Padmávati with her attendants closed the throng. They entered the cavern and there found security from dishonour and captivity in the devouring element.

A generous contest now arose between the Rana and his sorrowing son as to which should lead the fatal charge. The father prevailed and in obedience to his commands the son with a small band passed through the enemy's lines and reached the outer world in safety. Satisfied now that his line was not extinct, the Rana called around him his devoted clans for whom life had no longer any charms. They threw open the gates and with reckless despair carried death or met it in the hosts of Alla-ud-din's army.

The conqueror took possession of an inanimate capital, strewn with the bodies of the brave defenders. The smoke yet issued from the recesses where lay consumed the object of his desire. Since that awful day in A.D. 1303 the cavern has been sacred. No eye has penetrated its gloom, and superstition has placed as its guardian a huge serpent whose venomous breath extinguishes the light which might guide intruders to "the place of sacrifice." Alla-ud-din remained in Chittore some days, admiring the grandeur of his conquest, and committing every act of barbarity and wanton destruction which a bigoted zeal could suggest against the magnificent temples, palaces and other monuments of art. He spared, however, the beautiful palace of Padmávati which still stands in silent beauty, a sad memorial of her chequered life and of the woes innumerable of which she was the innocent cause.

A Mohammedan saint, Malik Muhammad, who lived 250 years afterwards, has made the life of this princess of Ceylon the theme of a great philosophical work called after her. It tells in vivid language the story of Ratan Sen's quest for her, of Alla-ud-din's ruthless siege, of Ratan Sen's valour, of Padmávati's wifely devotion, culminating in the terrible sacrifice of all in the cavern of fire. The poet-saint makes of these events an allegory describing the search of the soul for true wisdom and the trials and temptations which beset it in its course.

XIII.

Between the tenth and the fifteenth centuries the trade of the Island gradually passed into the hands of the Arabs, who became undisputed masters of the Indian seas. The trade was exceedingly valuable, and embraced not only pearls, gems, spices, and elephants, for which the Island was celebrated from remote times, but the products of Eastern and Southern Asia brought here by the Chinese to be exchanged for the wares brought by the Arabs from the countries beyond the Euphrates.

Arab adventurers settled on the Indian and Ceylon coasts, inter-married with the natives, and in time acquired great political influence over the Sinhalese king, who, reduced to impotence, reigned at Kotte, while the seaports were virtually in the hands of the Arabs, the northern half of the Island and the east coast (Jaffna, Vanni, Nuwarakalawiya, and Batticaloa) were ruled by Tamil kings, and petty chieftains held mimic court in different parts of the west and south.

Among the exports of the Island cinnamon was the most prized. It was a luxury so rare as to be a suitable gift for a king, so costly that a crown of cinnamon tipped with gold was a becoming offering to the gods. It is believed to have been originally obtained by the Arabs from Eastern Africa and to have gained a footing in India and afterwards in Ceylon where, favoured by natural conditions of climate and soil, the Ceylon variety became the most perfect sample and grew wild in the woods.

Strangely enough there is no reference to Ceylon cinnamon in the account of the travels of Marco Polo, who towards the end of the 13th century visited Ceylon on his homeward route to Venice from China, where he had for 17 years resided at the court of the Emperor Kubla Khan.

"And the king of this Island," says Marco Polo, "possesses a ruby which is the finest and biggest in the world. . . You must know the great Khan sent an embassy and begged the king as a favour greatly desired to sell him this ruby, offering to give him for it the ransom of a city or in fact what the king would. But the king replied that on no account whatever would he sell it, for it had come to him from his ancestors. Furthermore you must know that in the land of Seilan there is an exceeding high mountain. . . Now it befel that the great Khan heard how on that mountain there was the sepulchre of our first father Adam, and that some of his hair and of his teeth and the dish from which he used to eat were still preserved there. So he thought he would get hold of them somehow or another, and despatched a great embassy for the purpose in the year of Christ 1284. The ambassadors with a great company travelled on by sea and by land until they arrived at the Island of Seilan and presented themselves before the king, and they were so urgent with the king that they succeeded in getting two of his grinder teeth which were passing great and thick, and they also got some of the hair and the dish from which the great personage used to eat, which is of a very beautiful green porphyry" (Colonel Yule's *Travels of Marco Polo*, Vol. II., page 295).

The earliest reference to Ceylon cinnamon is by Ibn Batuta, the Moorish traveller from Tangiers, who visited Ceylon, 1347 A.D., on a pilgrimage to Adam's Peak. He landed at Puttalam and found the shore "covered with cinnamon wood which the merchants of Malabar transport without any other price than a few articles of clothing which are given as presents to the king. This may be attributed to the circumstance that it is brought down by the mountain torrents and left in great heaps upon the shore." He found the greatest king in the Island to be the Tamil king of Jaffna, Arya Chakravarti, who had a powerful fleet commanding the western coast and under whose protection he accomplished the pilgrimage to Adam's Peak viâ Chilaw and "Konakar" (? Kurunegala), extending his journey to the temple at "Dinaur" (Devinuwara or Dondra) and returning by way of "Kale" (Galle) and "Kolambu" (Colombo) which he calls "the finest and largest city in Serendib."

XIV.

Arya Chakravarti was the title of an old Tamil dynasty established in Jaffna, whose sway often extended over large portions of Ceylon. The founder of this dynasty is said by tradition to have been a blind minstrel from the Chola country of South India. Being blind, he depended for his subsistence on the earnings of his wife. One day he quarrelled with her and left home, saying he was going to Lanka (Ceylon). "Ah, you are going to Lanka," she said sneeringly, "to obtain a tusked elephant and a fertile land." On his arrival at the king's court, he was refused admittance to his presence, as it was deemed inauspicious for a king to see a blind man. It was however arranged that the king should stand behind a curtain and hear the minstrel's song. Unknown to him the king exchanged his royal robes for an archer's dress and stood bow in hand. The minstrel, divining the disguise, improvised this stanza, comparing him to Rama, the hero of the *Rámáyana*.

"O Aditya (meaning Rama) whose mighty arms stemmed the sea waves, why have thy hand assumed the bow? For prosperous Lanka has neither her king (meaning Ravana) nor the stag (meaning that which decoyed Rama away from Sita and left her alone to be carried off by Ravana) nor the seven *Mara* trees (meaning those which Rama shot through with a single arrow) for thee to shoot."

The king immediately laid aside the archer's garb and successively wore his queen's robes and his own. The minstrel composed *ex tempore* a lyric in ten stanzas to suit the different guises and sang it to the accompaniment of his lute. The king was greatly pleased with the minstrel and bestowed on him a tusked elephant and the peninsula of Jaffna, thus making true the ironical remark of his wife. The land was mostly uninhabited and covered with jungle, which he cleared with the aid of colonists imported from South India and converted into a rich country. From his professional name (*Yál-pánar*, the lute-minstrel), the land was called *Yál-pánam*, the Minstrel's Land. The Sinhalese changed the name into *Yápane*, which the British anglicised to *Jaffna.*

The minstrel invited from the continent a son of the Chola king and installed him as king under the name Sing-arya-chakravarti. The installation is said in the *Kailása Málai* to have occurred in the year 3,000 of the *Kali Yuga*, equal to 101 B.C. If this date be correct, the Ceylon king who patronized the minstrel was probably Pulattya, the Tamil who expelled Walagam Bahu (p. 21 *supra*) and ruled in his place at Anuradhapura. The capital of the kingdom of Jaffna was fixed at Nallur ('the good city'), and the kings soon became powerful rivals of the kings of Anuradhapura and Polonnaruwa. The north-western ports of Mantota and Kudiramalai (the *Hippuros* of Pliny), which from ancient times had been the ports of call of Greek, Roman, Arab, Indian and Chinese ships, served as the basis of a naval force which often gave the kings of Jaffna the command of the Ceylon seas and a predominant influence in the Island.

Between the kingdom of Jaffna and the Sinhalese kingdom of Anuradhapura lies a strip of country called the *Vanni*, bounded on the west and east by the sea and extending from Mannar to Trincomalie. This region was held by a tribe of Tamils called the *Vanniyar*, whose original settlement was Kottiyar in the Trincomalie district and who, spreading therefrom, formed themselves into little principalities each ruled by a prince or a princess. Some of these princesses were remarkable women and have been raised by posterity to divine honors. The inhabitants were of a martial spirit and frequently at war with the kings of the North and South. In the Dutch times a Vanni princess led with conspicuous bravery the popular resistance to the foreigner till she was taken prisoner. They were not finally subdued till the British established themselves in the Island.

The Vanniyar extended their influence into the Anuradhapura district, and their descendants constituted the highest caste among the Sinhalese and were known as the *Vannihuru*. The Assistant Government Agent of Anuradhapura, Mr. Brodie, in his diary (1851) quotes the Nikawewa Ratemahatmaya who belonged to this class: "The people respect the Vanniyar more than the Vellalas, but the former presuming on their superiority, neglect education and are falling into the back ground. We are not mere Vellalas: we came over with the *Aiyanar Dewiyo* [a sylvan deity much worshipped in these parts] long before the Bo-tree" [see p. 18 *supra. ad fin*]. Asked what he would do if one of the women of his caste married a Vellala, he replied: "In the Kandyan times we should have killed her at once. But now—humph!—well, I don't know what else we could do with her now either." The Vannihuru have now merged in the Vellalas.

The Sinhalese kings, subject to attacks from the Tamils established in the North and to Tamil invasions from South India, were in no enviable position. About

1288 Arya Chakravarti of Jaffna captured the Sinhalese capital of Yapahu (in the Kurunegala district) and carried off its most valued treasure, the tooth-relic of Buddha, and presented it to the Pandyan king of South India, from whom it was afterwards recovered by Parakrama Bahu III. by a peaceful mission. It was a later Arya Chakravarti of the same dynasty whom the traveller Ibn Batula mentions as the greatest king in the Island and under whose protection he completed his travels with security and comfort.

XV.

The power of this king was felt all over Ceylon, and the Sinhalese king at Gampola was ill-fitted to cope with him. The resistance of the Sinhalese people was headed by a man, alike remarkable as a warrior and statesman, the foremost figure in the history of Ceylon for the next half a century—Alakesvara or Alagakkonara, a Tamil prince from Kanchi, the ancient capital of the Chola kings, who had settled in Ceylon and intermarried with the royal house and was the *de facto* ruler of the land, though he held the rank only of *Prabhurája* or Viceroy. Contemporary historians and poets* speak in no measured terms of his services to the Sinhalese people and the Buddhist church.

His seat was at Raygama in the Kalutara district. It took him 20 years to complete his preparations against the mighty Arya Chakravarti. Having fortified and provisioned Raygama and the seaboard capital Kotte, then known as *Jayawardanapura* ('the city of victory'), and raised an adequate army, he hurled a challenge at Arya Chakravarti by hanging the tax collectors whom he had stationed in different parts of the country. The reply came in two great hosts, numbering over a hundred thousand, simultaneously attacking Gampola and Kotte. The Sinhalese

* *Mahawansa ; Nikaya Sangraha ; Attanagala Wansa ; Mayura Sandesa.*

king fled from Gampola to Raygama, but his brave troops defeated and dispersed the enemy. The force intended for the capture of Kotte was brought in ships and disembarked at Colombo and Panadure. Alakesvara himself took the field and inflicted a crushing defeat, which effectually broke Arya Chakravarti's power and paved the way for Jaffna shortly afterwards becoming a Sinhalese Province for a time.

Alakesvara, now become a national hero, administered the country with wisdom and vigour. He rescued the country from anarchy, purified the Buddhist church, summoning for the purpose a convocation over which he presided, patronized learning, adorned the cities with noble buildings and well deserved the affection of a grateful people.

About this time an event occurred which is ignored or slurred over in the Sinhalese chronicles. A Chinese Admiral arrived with a mandate from the Chinese Emperor (1408 A.D.) demanding tribute from Alakesvara or Alagakkonara, who in the Chinese chronicles is described as "Alee-ko-nae-wahr a native of Solee (Chola country in South India) and an adherent of the heterodox faith and who, so far from honouring Buddha, tyrannized over his followers." Alakesvara was thus apparently of the Brahminical religion,—a statement confirmed by a contemporary poem *Mayura Sandesa*, where he is described as "the friend of Mahesvara" (Siva). But it is not correct that he tyrannized over the Buddhists, who on the contrary found in him an enthusiastic patron and protector. "He was a mighty prince of great wisdom endued with majesty and faith and such like virtues," says the *Mahawansa*, "and desired greatly to promote the welfare of the church and the kingdom."

To avenge the defeat inflicted by Alakesvara the Chinese Emperor sent another expedition, which about 1412 succeeded by a night attack in capturing the king and taking him and his family to China.

Who the captive was, is not certain. He is called "Alibunar" and "Alee-ko-nae-wahr"; and the name Alagakkonara or Alakesvara was borne by many members of the royal family. The captive king may have been Wira Alakesvara *alias* Wijaya Bahu VI. In the 6th month of the year 1411, says the Chinese chronicle, the prisoners were presented at Court. The Chinese Emperor took pity on them and set them at liberty and ordered them to select a virtuous man from the royal family to occupy the throne. All the captives declared in favour of "See-ay-nae-na," and an envoy was sent with a seal to invest him with the royal dignity as a vassal of the Emperor. For fifty years afterwards the kings of Ceylon paid tribute to China. Another Chinese chronicle identifies "Seay-pa-næ-na" with "Pu-la-ko-ma Ba-zae-La-cha," in whom we seem to recognize Parakrama Bahu Raja, who as Parakrama Bahu VI. ruled with lustre at Kotte for about 50 years till A.D. 1462 (p. 35 *supra*) and whose glories are chanted by the poet Totagamuwa.

XVI.

At the close of this century the kings of Ceylon were threatened with danger from a new quarter. A Portuguese fleet, despatched from Goa to capture some ships of their Arab rivals in the Eastern trade, was carried by the current to the harbour of Galle (1505 A.D.). The Portuguese found Arab ships loading with cinnamon and, unable to prevent it, erected a stone cross at Galle as a memento of their arrival in the Island, and put to sea again.

Twelve years later, the Portuguese re-appeared in Ceylon, this time at Colombo. "It came to pass," says the chronicle (*Râjâvaliya*), "that in the month of April a ship from Portugal arrived in Colombo, and information was brought to the king that there was in the harbour a race of very white and beautiful people who wear boots and hats of iron and never stop in one place. They eat a sort of white stone and drink blood and they have guns with a noise louder than thunder, and a ball shot from one of them, after traversing a league, will break up a castle of marble."

With the assent of the king, Dharma Parakrama Bahu IX., the Portuguese erected a factory, which they afterwards converted into a fortress. They soon ousted from trade and power the Arabs, or Moors, as the Portuguese called them, identifying them, by reason of their religion, with the Moors who ruled the Spanish peninsula. The Sinhalese king soon repented of the imprudent concessions he had made to the Portuguese and endeavoured in vain to withdraw from his engagements. The Portuguese established themselves gradually all along the coast.

The policy of the Portuguese was governed by territorial ambition, commercial greed, and religious proselytism. Every pagan was looked on as an enemy of Portugal and of Christ. The policy was prosecuted with a bigotry and cruelty which would be incredible, if there was not the testimony of their own historians. They regarded the subversion of the Portuguese rule as a judgment from heaven. "Not only the poor soldiers went out to rob, but those Portuguese who were lords of villages added rapes and adulteries which obliged the people to seek the company of beasts on the mountains rather than be subject to the more beastly villainies of men." Children were thrown by soldiers on the points of spears and a governor bade them hark how the young cocks crew. Mothers were forced to pound their children betwixt mill-stones and then beheaded.*

* A lesson which Ceylon kings learnt and later used when punishing treason on the part of subjects who conspired with the foreigner against them: as *e.g.*, in the terrible punishment inflicted on the Ehalapola family by the last king of Kandy. The only thing to be said in palliation is that in all countries until recently cruel punishments used to be inflicted on traitors and their families, treason being deemed almost a sacrilege and being at the same time given a very wide interpretation. The common law punishment in England was to draw the offender on the ground to the gallows, hang him by the neck, cut him down alive, take out his entrails while he was yet alive and burn them, to cut off his head and divide his body into four parts, the head and quarters to be at the disposal of the Crown. If the offender was a woman, she was burned alive.

Under the auspices of the Portuguese Christianity gained a footing in the northern and north-western coasts, chiefly by the zeal of the missionaries under the direction of Saint Francis Xavier, the great "Apostle of the Indies," whose tomb at Goa, the capital of Portuguese India, is periodically the scene of an imposing pilgrimage. The descendants of his converts form the vast majority of the Christian population of the Island.

During this period the three most magnificent temples in Ceylon were ruthlessly destroyed and plundered: in 1552, the temple of Siva at Sitawaka, described by a Portuguese historian as a structure of marvellous work on the building of which two thousand men had been continuously employed for twenty years; in 1587, the temple of Vishnu at Dondra, then the most sumptuous in Ceylon, built on vaulted arches on a promontory over-looking the sea, with towers elaborately carved and covered with plates of gilded brass, and covering so large an extent that to the Portuguese invaders "it was like a handsome city with a circuit of a full league"; and in 1622, "the temple of a thousand columns" sacred to Siva on the rock known as Sami rock overlooking the magnificent harbour of Trincomalee. Here, though the temple no longer stands nor the shrine, troops of worshippers gather almost daily and celebrate the ancient rites under the blue vault of the sky with melodious chants and lights and offerings of flower and fruit, incense and camphor, ending by casting them into the deep waters below unto the Unseen God.

In 1560 A.D., the most sacred object of Buddhist worship, the Daladá or Tooth-relic of Buddha, fell into the hands of the Portuguese. It had an eventful history. Rescued from the flames on the cremation of Gautama Buddha at Kusinara (about 540 B.C.), it was preserved for 800 years in Kalinga. About 310 A.D., when the king of that country was about to engage in a doubtful conflict, he despatched the precious relic to Ceylon in the charge of his daughter, concealed in the folds of her hair. The grateful king and people of the Island established its worship on a magnificent scale at Anuradhapura, and afterwards at Polonnaruwa when the capital was transferred there. After the relic had remained about a thousand years in Ceylon, it was captured by Arya Chakravarti (p. 47 *supra*) and taken back to South India. It was recovered by the diplomacy of Parakrama Bahu III. and brought to Polonnaruwa. During the troublous times that followed, it was hidden in different parts of the Island, and finally came into the possession of the Tamil kings of Jaffna, from whom it was taken by the Portuguese on the capture of Jaffna. They carried it to Goa and rejecting offers of vast treasure by the Buddhist king of Pegu, reduced it to ashes. Soon afterwards a copy, or as the Buddhists claim, the original itself,—the destroyed tooth being a counterfeit,—was set up, which is enshrined at the chief temple at Kandy, the Dalada Maligawa, and draws worshippers from all Buddhist lands.

XVII.

The Sinhalese capital Kotte being almost within the range of the Portuguese guns at Colombo, the Sinhalese king was unable to resist the arrogant demands of the Portuguese. Alarmed by the indignation of his own subjects at repeated concessions to the Portuguese, he was compelled to draw closer the alliance with them. In order to gain the favour of his patrons, he and his courtiers embraced Christianity and adopted Portuguese names. This fashion was largely followed on the coast, and we see the result in the large number of Portuguese names which continue to puzzle the visitors to the Island. In 1540 a mission was sent to Lisbon with a statue of the king's grandson and a golden crown with which

KINGS OF THE SULUVANSA OR LOWER DYNASTY, FROM 1037 to 1505 A.D.

No.	Name.	Date of Accession.	Capital.	Length of Reign.*
	(*Interregnum of 12 Years*)	A.D. 1038—1049	Polonnaruwa and Ruhuna ...	
115	Kirti (Tamil)	1049	Ruhuna ...	8 days
116	Mahalana Kirti (Tamil) ...	1049	,, ...	3
117	Vikum Pandi or Vikrama Pandi (Tamil) ...	1052	Kalutara ...	1
118	Jagat Pala (Tamil) ...	1053	Ruhuna ...	4
119	Parakrama or Perakum (Tamil)	1057	,, ...	2
120	Lokesvara (Tamil) ...	1059	Kataragama ...	6
121	Vijaya Bahu I. or Siri Sangabo IV.	1065	Polonnaruwa and Anuradhapura	55
122	Jaya Bahu I.	1120	Polonnaruwa ...	1
123	Vikrama Bahu I. ...	1121	,, ...	21
124	Gaja Bahu II ...	1142	,, ...	22
125	Parakrama Bahu I. the Great	1164	,, ...	33
126	Vijaya Bahu II. ...	1197	,, ...	1
127	Mahinda VI. (Tamil)	1198	,, ...	5 days
128	Kirti Nissanka Malla do.	1198	,, ...	9
129	Vira Bahu I. do.	1207	,, ...	1 day
130	Vikrama Bahu II. do.	1207	,, ...	3 mths.
131	Codaganga do.	1207	,, ...	9 mths.
132	Lilavati (*Queen*) ...	1208	,, ...	3
133	Sahasamalla do.	1211	,, ...	2
134	Kalyanavati (*Queen*) do.	1213	,, ...	6
135	Dharmasoka	1219	,, ...	1
136	Anikanga	1220	,, ...	17 days
132	Lilavati (*restored*) ...	1220	,, ...	1
137	Lokesvara (Tamil) ...	1221	,, ...	9 mths.
132	Lilavati (*restored*) ...	1221	,, ...	7 mths.
138	Parakrama Pandu (Tamil)	1222	,, ...	3
139	Māgha Kalinga do.	1225	,, ...	21
140	Vijaya Bahu III. ...	1246	Dambadeniya ...	4
141	Parakrama Bahu II. or Kalikāla Sāhitya Sarvagna PanditaParakrama Bahu	1250	,, ...	35
142	Vijaya Bahu IV. or Bosat Vijaya Bahu ...	1285	Polonnaruwa ...	2
143	Bhuvaneka Bahu I. ...	1287	Polonnaruwa and Yapahu ...	11
144	Parakrama Bahu III. ...	1290	Polonnaruwa ...	5
145	Bhuvaneka Bahu II. ...	1303	Kurunegala ...	2
146	Parakrama Bahu IV. ...	1305	,, ...	—
147	Bhuvaneka Bahu III. ...	—	,, ...	—
148	Jaya Bahu I. ...	—	,, ...	—
149	Bhuvaneka Bahu IV. ...	1347	Gampola ...	14
150	Parakrama Bahu V. ...	1361	,, ...	10
151	Vikrama Bahu III. ...	1371	,, ...	7
152	Bhuvaneka Bahu V. ...	1378	Kotte ...	20
153	Vira Bahu II.	1398	,, ...	12
154	Parakrama Bahu VI. ...	1410	,, ...	52
155	Jaya Bahu II. ...	1462	,, ...	2
156	Bhuvaneka Bahu VI. ...	1464	,,	7
157	Pandita Parakrama Bahu VII.	1471	,, ...	14
158	Vira Parakrama Bahu VIII. ...	1485	,, ...	20
159	Dharma Parakrama Bahu IX.	1505	,, ...	22
160	Vijaya Bahu V. ...	1527	,, ...	7 years
161	Bhuvaneka Bahu VII. ...	1534	,, ...	8
	Māyadunu	—	Sitavaka ...	—
162	Don Juan Dharmapala ...	1542	Kotte ...	39
163	Raja Sinha I.	1581	Sitavaka ...	11
164	Vimala Dharma Suriya I.	1592	Kandy ...	12
165	Senerat	1604	,, ..	30
166	Raja Sinha II. ...	1634	,, ...	50
167	Vimala Dharma Suriya II.	1684	,, ...	22
168	Vira Parakrama Narendra Sinha	1706	,, ...	33
169	Siri Vijaya Raja Sinha (Tamil)	1739	,, ...	8
170	Kirti Sri Raja Sinha (Tamil)	1747	,, ...	33
171	Rajadhi Raja Sinha do.	1780	,, ...	18
172	Sri Vikrama Raja Sinha (Tamil)	1798—1815	.. ...	17

* In years, unless otherwise stated.

the statue was to be crowned in recognition of his right to succeed the king. This was done with great pomp by the Portuguese king, but scarcely improved the position of his protégé.

The masses of the people loathed the pusillanimous policy of their kings and maintained a heroic struggle for 150 years against the foreigner till he was expelled. At first greatly handicapped through ignorance of the use of firelocks and gunpowder, it was not long before they excelled the Portuguese in the manufacture of muskets. Among the leaders of this great national movement Mayadunne and his son Rajasinha, "the lion-king" of Sitawaka and Rajasinha II. of Kandy, will ever hold honoured places in the grateful recollections of their countrymen.

Sitawaka, though its name has disappeared from modern maps and is lost in that of Avisawella, is a place of romantic and historical interest. Here, in prehistoric times, Sita, the heroine of the *Ramayana*, was forcibly carried by Ravana. The place derives its name from her and seems still fragrant with her memory. During the middle ages when, according to tradition, Ceylon was split into 16 kingdoms, the ruler of Sitawaka was acknowledged as overlord by the others, being deemed of purer blood and of the royal Indian stock. A yearly festival was held here, at which all the princes assembled. It lasted 16 days, a day for each prince, and at the close a golden bracelet, engraved with 16 heads, was brought out of the temple and presented to the overlord. This mark of homage gradually fell into disuse. But even after Sitawaka had ceased to be a separate kingdom, the kings of Kandy and Uva found it expedient to conciliate the popular sentiment by undergoing the formal ceremony of inauguration in the ancient palace on the bank of the Sitawaka river.

It was this city which Mayadunne rebuilt in 1534 and established as the centre of his fief which covered the Three and Four Korales and Dinawaka and of the national resistance to the policy of his pusillanimous brother Bhuvaneka Bahu VI. of Kotte. Raygama, the seat of Alakesvara (p. 47 *supra*), again rose into prominence at this time through its brave ruler, Raygam Bandara, brother and ally of Mayadunne, and passed to him on the former's death. After a protracted war in which Sitawaka was more than once captured and given to the flames and Mayadunne was driven into forest retreats only to emerge once more undaunted, a combined army of Europeans and Sinhalese was defeated in 1563 by his youthful son Rajasinha and pursued to the walls of Colombo. He laid siege to Kotte with vigour, reducing its inhabitants to the verge of starvation. The alarmed Portuguese commander in anticipation of a long siege caused the flesh of those killed in battle to be salted as a provision against famine. In the following year Kotte was finally abandoned, and the Portuguese retired to their fort in Colombo, taking with them the unfortunate king, who thence forward lived there, "tormented," says the Portuguese historian Faria Y Souza, "no less by the covetousness of the Portuguese commander than he had been before by the tyranny of Rajasinha."

In 1581 Rajasinha succeeded his father. Immediately on his accession he had to meet an attempt by the Portuguese to gain possession of Sitawaka. Marching to oppose them as far as Hewagama, he sent Wikramasinha Mudaliar to hold the enemy in check at Mulleriyawa. Despite a desperate resistance, the general was driven back upon the main army. Rajasinha put his whole force in motion and advanced to Mulleriyawa. Detaching a body of a thousand trained soldiers to take the Portuguese in the rear, he led the attack in front with his elephants, another thousand Ulangan spearmen and the Radágé companies of Alutkuru and Hewagam Korales. Then ensued one of the hardest fought battles of Ceylon history. It was only his marvellous energy and daring that turned it from imminent defeat into complete victory. Riding through the ranks and animating them by his presence and encouragement, he at once closed with the Portuguese in order to minimise the effect of their fire. But the impetuosity of his troops yielded to the disciplined fire of the Portuguese, and Rajasinha saw his soldiers slowly giving way. "The king", says the *Rajavaliya*, "would not permit his army to retreat", but again urging them on, at length drove a way into the midst of the Portuguese. These, unable longer to load their guns, clubbed them and met the foe hand to hand. So desperate grew the struggle that Portuguese and Sinhalese alike clung to the tails of the elephants and fought. The king on horseback flew from side to side, encouraging here, threatening there. "That day blood flowed like water on the field of Mulleriyawa." The Portuguese, pressed in flank and rear, could not retreat and left 1,600 killed on the battle field.

Within a few years Rajasinha gradually extended his dominions and made himself master of nearly all Ceylon, and the Portuguese were confined to their forts on the coast and even there were almost at his mercy. In 1586 Rajasinha laid siege to Colombo with an army of 50,000 men supported by a naval force. He was, however, called away by an insurrection fostered by the Portuguese. He died in 1592, at an advanced age, of a wound received in battle. "Since my eleventh year," he said as he neared his death, "I have been fighting. No king was able to stand against me, but he who has appeared in the hill country this time is a favourite of fortune; the power of my merits has declined." Thus died king Rajasinha who, as the chronicle says, "had reduced this beautiful Lanka under one canopy."

"In the character of Rajasinha I.", says Pridham, "courage and ability were strangely blended with ferocity and cunning. At the advanced age of 100 years he retained much of the energy and elasticity and energy of youth. The lesson acquired under his father's reign, that Europeans were only to be repelled by an altered system of native warfare, was duly put in force, and resulted in the success it deserved......... Nurtured under other and different influences, Rajasinha, while equally protecting the liberties of his country, might have devoted a portion of his genius and energy to healing the wounds gaping from every part of its social and political being...........He had some taste for literature and patronized men of genius.

"By religion a Brahmin, Rajasinha was not the prince to protect, and scarcely to tolerate, the religion of Buddha, whose sacred books he destroyed and whose priests he degraded or extirpated while exalting those of his own communion. Hence it is that the Buddhist and Christian historians who had equal cause to hate his memory—the former in his character as a persecutor, the latter in his career as their successful opponent—have combined to traduce a monarch whom, while loathing for his cruelty and treachery, the European cannot fail to respect for qualities and impulses in general confined in their origin to sources supposed to exist only in the bracing temperature of a northern clime."

The struggle against the Portuguese was continued with unabated vigour by his successors now seated at the hill capital of Kandy, (*Senkadagala* as it was called), and especially by Rajasinha II. who ruled over Ceylon for 50 years (1637-87). While yet heir-apparent, he inflicted a crushing defeat on the Portuguese viceroy, Constantine de Sa, in Wellawaya in the district of Badulla (1630). Not a Portuguese soldier escaped and the head of the brave commander, carried on a drum, was presented to Rajasinha. "This unfortunate day," says the Portuguese historian Ribeyro, "commenced our ruin in the Island of

Ceylon." The Kandyans, flushed by this signal victory, followed it up by a march on Colombo, which was only saved from their hands by the timely arrival of assistance from Goa. Seven years later Rajasinha inflicted a not less disastrous blow, at Balana, on the Portuguese under General de Melho.

XVIII.

The first Dutch ships were seen in Ceylon waters in 1602, commanded by Admiral Van Spilbergen, and the Sinhalese kings were glad to accept the offer of the Dutch alliance in their war against Portugal. But though the Portuguese were finally driven out, the Dutch did not prove more faithful allies. Rajasinha II., in his letters which are extant* and which at times polite to excess, at others blaze out into fierce anger, often bitterly regretted having invited the Dutch to Ceylon.

Of Rajasinha II., we have an excellent account from the pen of Robert Knox in his *Historical Relation of the Island of Ceylon* published in the reign of Charles II. Knox and his father, sailing in their good ship *Ann* of the East India Company from Madras, were overtaken by a storm and had to put in for repairs at Kottiyar, in the Trincomalee district. They were captured and sent to the king who had a strange fancy for detaining foreigners. Knox's father died in captivity at Bandarakoswatte in Kurunegala district in 1661, and Knox himself escaped after a captivity of 20 years borne with exemplary fortitude to write his famous book, admirable alike for careful observation, tenacious memory and simple truthfulness.

The policy of the Dutch was peaceful, and their ruling principle the monopoly of trade in spices. They developed cultivation, improved the means of

* Correspondence between Rajasinha II., and the Dutch, by Donald Ferguson, the *Colombo R. A. S. Journal*, Vol. 18, No. 55.

communication, especially by canals, and established a lucrative trade with the interior. Cinnamon was the staple export. It was "the Helen or bride of contest" (as Baldæus called it) for whose exclusive possession successive European invaders had in turn contended.

For the peeling and preparation of this precious bark the Portuguese had utilized the Salágama caste, of whom Sir Alexander Johnston, Chief Justice of Ceylon, gives an interesting account in a paper contributed by him to the Royal Asiatic Society of Great Britain, of which he was Vice-President (vol. III. of the *R. A. S. Journal.*) The Sinhalese inhabitants of Ceylon were, previous to the thirteenth century, ignorant of the art of weaving fine cloth, and their kings offered great rewards to any subject who would bring over weavers from India for the purpose of some introducing that art to Ceylon. Early in the thirteenth century a Moor of Beruwala, in the Kalutara district, tempted by the offer, brought over from India eight weavers. The king received them with great kindness, had them married to women of distinction, gave them houses and lands, established a manufactory for them in the vicinity of the palace, and conferred high honours upon their chief.

The descendants of these people, having, in the course of two centuries, become numerous and powerful, excited the jealousy of the Kandyan Government, and were compelled by the king, as punishment for some alleged offence against his authority, to quit the interior and settle near the South-west coast, where cinnamon grew to perfection, and to peel and prepare for the Government without pay as much cinnamon annually as it might require. The Dutch continued the system and rewarded the cinnamon cultivators with many privileges.

About 1770, driven by the Sinhalese king's obstruction to the collection of cinnamon from his forests, the Dutch officials conceived the happy idea, in opposition to the universal prejudice in favour of wild-growing cinnamon, of cultivating the plant. The attempt proved a complete success. The whole European demand was thus supplied by the Dutch, who would even burn the cinnamon in Holland lest its abundance should reduce the price. They made the peeling of cinnamon, save by the appointed officer, the selling or exporting of a single stick, or wilful injury to a plant, a capital offence. The monopoly was continued under the English rule till it was abolished in 1833.

In 1740 Governor Van Imhoff, by a system of forced labour, planted the waste land along the coast south of Colombo with the cocoa palm. This was the beginning of that almost unbroken grove of palms which for 100 miles line the South-west shore. To the Dutch also was due the introduction of the coffee plant, which, though it failed to bring them profit, contributed very materially to the prosperity of the Island during the greater part of the period of the British rule.

XIX.

The British appeared on the scene at the close of the eighteenth century. In 1782, when great Britain was at war with Holland, the English East India Company despatched a force for the reduction of the Dutch possessions in Ceylon. The force landed at Trincomalee, which, after a little resistance, capitulated, and an ambassador was sent to the king to propose a treaty of peace, which the latter declined. The ambassador, on his return to Trincomalee, found that the French, who also were at war with the British at the time, had surprised the fort and carried off the British garrison. Trincomalee was restored to the Dutch by the French in the following year.

In 1795, when war broke out afresh between the Sinhalese and the Dutch, the king solicited the aid of the British. A British armament was accordingly despatched to his assistance from Madras. The Dutch offered little resistance, and in 1796 all places in the occupation of the Dutch were ceded to the British, and in 1802, by the treaty of Amiens, were formally transferred to Great Britain.

The Dutch name will live in Ceylon as long as the Roman-Dutch law, which they introduced and which is virtually the common law of this Island. The Dutch descendants are among the most educated and useful members of the Island population, and form the upper stratum of the "Burgher" community of Ceylon, the lower stratum consisting of Portuguese descendants and Eurasians.

The Dutch garrisons consisted of Malays and Caffirs imported for military service. Among the former were descendants of Malay princes and their attendants deported hither from Java for political reasons. The Malays in Ceylon still retain some of the old military instinct. The Caffirs were imported from Mozambique and other parts of the African coast. Though as many as 9,000 were at different times imported into the Island, they had become so merged in the native population that even in the early years of the last century they could, according to a contemporary writer Bertolacci, hardly be distinguished.

The territory ceded by the Dutch was from 1797 to 1802 placed under the English East India Company, and formed a part of the territory of the Government of Madras until 1802, when Ceylon was created a Crown Colony. In 1815 the British Government declared war against the last king of Kandy. Mr. Sawers, who was the chief British official in Kandy from 1815 to 1827, says in his *Notes on the Conquest of Kandy:* "It has been frequently stated that the king had by his tyranny forfeited the loyalty and attachment of the great body of the people, but this imputation is not well-founded. His quarrels were with his chiefs and the chiefs alone; and perhaps the circumstance which particularly rendered him obnoxious to the hatred of the chiefs, was the disposition he evinced of a determination to protect the people from the oppression of the aristocracy." Their resentment made them co-operate with the British army and crippled his defence, and he was eventually taken prisoner.

The report of the capture reached the Governor and Commander-in-chief, General Brownrigg, while he was at dinner with a small party of officers. One of them thus describes the scene. "The intelligence being highly gratifying and in many respects of the utmost importance, His Excellency became greatly affected. He stood up at table and, while the tears rolled down his cheeks, shook hands with every one present, and thanked them for their exertions in furtherance of an object which seemed to be nearly accomplished and which had been vainly attempted for nearly three centuries by three European powers in succession—the conquest of the kingdom of Kandy" (Marshall's *Ceylon* p. 158.)

In terms of a convention held on 2nd March, 1815, at Kandy, between the British authorities and the Kandyan chiefs, the king was dethroned, and the Sinhalese voluntarily surrendered their Island to the British Sovereign with full reservation of their rights and liberties. They may thus claim to be one of the few ancient races of the world who have not been conquered. The Kandyan king was conveyed to Colombo and deported thence to Vellore in the Madras Presidency, where he died in 1832 of dropsy.

XX.

Thus ended the oldest dynasty in the world, after enduring for twenty-four centuries, and the whole Island passed under the sway of Britain. A few years ago, at Tanjore in the Madras Presidency, I had the honor of being presented to the last surviving Queen of Kandy. In spite of straitened means she still maintained the traditions and ceremonial of a court. Speaking from behind a curtain, she was pleased to welcome me and to express her appreciation of some little services rendered to her family since their downfall. She has now passed away. A lineal descendant of the kings of Ceylon holds a minor clerkship in the Registrar-General's Department of this Island,—a living testimony to the revolutions of the wheel of fortune.

Over the garden gate of my old college (Christ's) at Cambridge—the college of Milton and of Darwin—stands the motto of the noble foundress, the Lady Margaret Beaufort, mother of Henry VII. The motto is *Souvent me souvient:* "it often comes to my mind," "often I am reminded." It is a perpetual reminder to successive generations of her family and her college of her ancestors' loyalty to duty, to king and country, and to high ideals. Well would it be for us Ceylonese if we too kept fresh in our hearts the great deeds done and the great ideals cherished by our ancestors, and strove to make ourselves worthy of our inheritance.

INDEX.